votional
Tony Evans and Chrystal Evans Hurst

nily book published by Tyndale House Publishers, Inc., Carol
188

ontributors: Margot Starbuck and Marianne Hering
ign by Jennifer Ghionzoli

ng-in-Publication data for this book is available by contacting the Library of
s at http://www.loc.gov/help/contact-general.html.

78-1-62405-122-7

in China

5 6 7 8 9 / 19 18 17 16 15 14 13

TON

CHRYSTA

KIN

WO

DEVOT

DAI

EMB

POW

TYNDALE HOUSE PUBLISHERS,

CAROL STREAM, ILLINOIS

A Focus on the Fa

Stream, Illinois 60

Focus on the Fam

trademarks of Fo

TYNDALE and

Tyndale House P

All Scripture qu

New Internation

Used by permis

com). Scripture

Version®, (ESV

News Publishe

marked (HCSB)

1999, 2000, 2

Scripture quo

quotations m

Copyright ©

Used by per

All italics in

Editorial

Cover de

Photogra

All rights

Image o

Catalog

Congre

ISBN

Printe

1 2 3

Contents

Introduction

When a kingdom woman's alarm sounds each morning, the devil tries to hit her snooze button. He'll do whatever he can to try to stop her from taking on a new day with the mind of God. But a kingdom woman won't stop doing all she can for God's kingdom until she makes the devil regret ever messing with her.

Begin each morning kingdom-woman ready with these 90 devotions written to prepare you for the life of good works God has in store for you (Ephesians 2:10). Each entry has a theme taken from the inspiring pages of *Kingdom Woman* that will encourage you to live a life that makes a difference. You'll find challenging biblical nuggets from Dr. Tony Evans as well as snippets of wisdom from Chrystal Evans Hurst's *Chrystal's Chronicles*.

The gospel of Mark says, "To you has been given the secret of the kingdom of God" (4:11 ESV). *Kingdom Woman Devotional* will help you uncover the secret to kingdom living so you can share it with your family, church, and community.

1

Kingdom Women Listen to God

Listening to God's voice is the secret of the assurance that He will listen to mine.

—Andrew Murray, *With Christ in the School of Prayer*

Do you feel as if a kingdom woman was *someone else*? Have you *wanted* to be her but felt you weren't faithful enough or determined enough? Take heart! That voice in your head whispering, "You're not enough . . ." is *not* God's voice! Rather, your heavenly Father encourages, "You can do this." He confirms, "You're not alone." And He offers, "Let's do it together." Like the father who smiles on his daughter, who prepares her to be all she's been made to be, God is encouraging and equipping you to thrive. As you begin this series of devotions, listen for that voice.

Listening to God's voice mutes the lies that disparage the value of kingdom women. Listening to God rejects a culture that says, "Women are weak and powerless." It contradicts the thought that women are second-class. It refutes the misconception that women must be subservient to men. The kingdom woman recognizes the devil's lies and deactivates them with the truth of God's Word.

Application

1. What specific ways has the enemy tried to convince you that you're not enough? In contrast, what does the voice of God say about your value and your mission?

2. Today, what Scripture will you hold in your heart to prepare you to face the challenges of this day?

Prayer

God, today I disagree with the enemy's lie that I'm inferior, that I'm not enough. I stand on the truth that You have equipped me with everything I need to be a kingdom woman. Amen.

2

Kingdom Women Are Created in God's Image

No one can make you feel inferior without your consent.

—Eleanor Roosevelt

A kingdom woman is created in the very image of God (Genesis 1:27). You were tenderly fashioned by God and are entirely worthy. Though the enemy will tell you that you are *not enough*, you *are already enough in Christ.* As you grow to become the kingdom woman God made you to be, the most important accessory in your spiritual purse is the truth about who God says you are. This truth is the deepest reality about who you are and dispels the enemy's lies.

This isn't to say that the kingdom woman is perfect. She doesn't live a life free of cares and concerns. She still faces the same challenges and temptations as other women. She still puts on her cute red stilettos one at a time! But by agreeing with God's vision of her, she lives in the reality of who God has made her to be. Each morning she chooses to fulfill her role as a woman of purpose. Satan has no power over a woman who disagrees with his schemes. He cannot make her feel inferior. In fact today, kingdom woman, he'd better watch his back.

Application

1. In what ways have you felt you don't measure up as a kingdom woman?

2. How does God see you and every kingdom woman? How are you made in His image?

Prayer

God, this day I will see myself as You see me—a kingdom woman formed in Your image. Help me to understand fully what that means, and empower me to fulfill Your purpose. Amen.

3

The Story That Is True

Every man's life is a fairy tale
written by God's fingers.
—Hans Christian Andersen

Some of the earliest stories our parents read to us, as children, were fairy tales. Whether the nineteenth-century Grimm brothers' versions or the twenty-first-century Disney versions, stories of noble princes and princesses who battle evil captured our hearts and minds and imaginations. They touched something inside us that longed for *our* lives to make a difference, to matter.

In the kingdom Jesus ushered in, we have become players in the story that continues to unfold. We aren't laboring mice who stitch a dress for a princess. We aren't the small underground diamond miners who keep house with an undercover princess. No, in the kingdom of God, we're the *actors*. The movers. We are the ones who exercise authority in the name of the King.

When we pursue justice on behalf of the poor

and marginalized, we exercise dominion. We do it when we welcome a stranger or befriend a sinner. We do it when we teach others what God is like.

Allow your life to be written by the fingers of God, confident that you've been created and called to rule with Him. There is one *Lord God, Yahweh*, Master and Ruler. As you position yourself under His authority, you are equipped to live out your unique purpose as a kingdom woman.

Application

1. When you were a girl, or now as a woman, what was your favorite fairy tale? In it do you hear echoes of God's story?

2. How will you, as a kingdom woman, exercise dominion this week by serving as an agent of God's rule?

Prayer

God, You are the one true Ruler of all. Help me hear Your voice that calls me to partner with You, and give me courage to respond faithfully. Amen.

4

She Is Not Somebody Else

Where is this woman—who is this woman—
who regularly and consistently positions
herself under and operates according to
God's complete rule over her life? Oh,
I know. She must be my neighbor.
—Chrystal Evans Hurst, *Kingdom Woman*

When you think about living as a mighty kingdom woman, do you share Chrystal's suspicion that this woman is someone else? If you do, you might also assume that she's the woman who sits next to you at church. She's the church mother who's been widowed forty-two years and whose faith in God's provision hasn't wavered. She's the woman who stitches her children's fine clothes. She's the one who doesn't struggle with temptations to drink or overeat. Whoever she is, she's *someone else*. (Satan is clever at dragging us off course, isn't he?)

We get in a bind both when we fall for the temptation to think *more* of ourselves than we should and when we think *less* of ourselves than we should! When we do, we agree with the enemy's deception. Chrystal confirms, "I'm so glad I don't have to aspire to be anyone else other than that woman God wants me to be."

Beloved kingdom woman, you are "God's workmanship" (Ephesians 2:10). You aren't *meant* to serve like the woman who sits beside you in church or like the one who sings solos in the choir or like the pastor's wife from another church in town. You are meant to rule according to the unique gifts and strengths and calling God has given *you.*

Application

1. Are you ever tempted to believe that the kingdom woman is someone *other* than you? Who are some of these women in your life?

2. God has entrusted you with particular gifts to build His kingdom. What are they? How can you use them in your life today?

Prayer

Father God, I confess that, too often, I don't look upon other women rightly, and I don't see myself as You see me. Give me Your vision to live as a kingdom woman. Amen.

5

A Funny Little Word

God calls the first woman ezer—a name that is used most frequently in the Old Testament for God himself.

—Carolyn Custis James, *Half the Church*

If there is one word that could describe the focal point of a kingdom woman's life, it would be *Christlike*. A second word that identifies the ministry of a kingdom woman is the Hebrew word *ezer*. The funny-sounding little word used in Genesis to identify the first woman, traditionally translated into English as "a suitable helper,"[1] has guided many a kingdom woman and her ministry.

As English speakers, we think we know what a "helper" is. A helper is the child who delivers a note from his teacher to the principal's office. A helper is the preadolescent who prepares dinner before her parents return home from work. A helper is the maid or gardener hired to do the dirty work no one in the household wants to do or has time to do.

In Hebrew, however, *ezer* means something categorically different. It challenges our ideas about a woman being a weak helper because it means "*strong* helper." By naming the woman as an *ezer*, God identified her with His own nature! God's *ezer* character describes the One who faithfully defends the weak (Psalm 33:20). God as *ezer* rescues the poor and needy (Psalm 70:5). God's people placed their confidence in the certainty that their help, their *ezer*, was in the name of the Lord (Psalm 124:8). The *ezer* is not a weak helper at all. Rather, the woman who identifies herself as *ezer* is mighty in power!

Application

1. In your own family, were women viewed as weak or strong?

2. Does the biblical description of woman, identifying her—you!—with God's mighty power, change the way you understand yourself today?

Prayer

Yahweh, You are a mighty helper to those in need. You are the ultimate Ezer, *who rescues and redeems. Make me more like You. Amen.*

6

Turning the World Right Side Up

[Where] did your Christ come from? From God and a woman! Man had not'ing to do with Him.

—Isabella Baumfree, nineteenth-century abolitionist and evangelist

Isabella Baumfree may be the most powerful kingdom woman you've never heard of. Born into slavery in New York, "Belle" escaped to freedom with her infant daughter in 1826. Together they found shelter with the Van Wagener family, who paid off Belle's owner, securing her safety. Belle came to know the Lord and became a devout Christian with an itinerant speaking ministry. In 1851 she addressed the Ohio Women's Rights Convention, where she delivered her now-famous speech "Ain't I a Woman?" *Now* you know who the kingdom woman is! She's the famous preacher and abolitionist Sojourner Truth, who said, "If the first woman God ever made was strong enough to turn the world upside down all alone, these women together ought to be able to turn it back, and get it right side up again!"[1]

Against all odds, Sojourner Truth didn't accept her culture's definition of *woman*. Rather, she was instructed and informed by the Word of God. In the face of innumerable hardships, she allowed herself to be transformed by God's purposes for her life.

Do you believe that God has called and equipped you to move in power as He called and equipped Sojourner Truth? While God won't call you in exactly the same way, God does call you to exercise, within your sphere of influence, the unique gifts He has given you. Through Christ in you, God is turning this world right side up again.

Application

1. What types of messages about what it meant to be a woman in the early 1800s do you imagine Isabella Baumfree heard?

2. What obstacle in your own life is God inviting you not only to overcome—to live as a powerful kingdom woman—but to empower others to overcome as well?

Prayer

God, thank You for the witness of Sojourner Truth, as well as the mighty army of kingdom women who have marched to the beat of Your drum. Give me courage to follow! Amen.

7

Unlikely Heroes

Kingdom women throughout
the Bible saved lives and nations.

—Tony Evans, *Kingdom Woman*

Shayne Moore, living in the suburbs of Chicago, was the average American "soccer mom." (In other parts of the country, this would be a "hockey mom" or a "basketball mom"!) She baked cupcakes, drove a minivan, and washed uniforms. In the midst of her normal life, however, Shayne's eyes were opened to a world in need. Unlike other folks, though, who have an eye-opening weeklong missions experience, at the nudging of the Holy Spirit, Shayne's eyes *stayed* open. While her kids were at school—and when they were underfoot!—she began advocating for those trapped in the web of poverty, HIV-AIDS, and human trafficking. With her laptop and cell phone, she responded to God's call by making a few of her own and writing books (*Global Soccer Mom* and *Refuse to Do Nothing*) on behalf of the ones God loves.

Too often we shortchange God and ourselves by assuming He will choose to work only through the powerful people in this world. We reason, "Deborah was a judge. Esther was a queen. Mary was divinely hand-picked by God!" The truth is, though, that God uses women like Shayne, who fold laundry and punch time cards and serve at church, to save lives and save nations. God uses women—mothers and wives and single women, young and old—to rescue a world in need.

Application

1. Who are some of the more well-known and noteworthy modern women to whom you can point and affirm, "God uses *that* woman"?

2. Now, identify a few of the less-heralded women God has called to use their particular giftings to build the kingdom. Are you one?

Prayer

God, I believe that I am among the kingdom women whom You have chosen to bless this world You love. Use me to show Your saving grace today. Amen.

8

What We Do Not Yet See

Oh, God of Dust and Rainbows, / help us to see / that without the dust the rainbow / would not be.

—Langston Hughes, *The Poems*, 1957–1967

When people are gathered at backyard barbecues or near a wooded area, they'll often encounter mosquitoes. One person will slap at his arm. Another will scratch her neck. Parents will spray repellent on children. Eventually someone will blame mosquitoes on *God*. Someone will demand, "What was God thinking when He made mosquitoes?!"

We often wonder the same thing about the circumstances in our lives. Why did God allow this to happen? Why didn't God prevent that? What could God be thinking? The truth is, we don't always know. God's thoughts are not our thoughts and His ways are not our ways (Isaiah 55:8). And although we don't understand, we do know that the same week God created mosquitoes, God also created Adam and Eve! The hands that made a human being from dust are the same ones that put rainbows in the sky.

Today, which God will you see?

Application

1. Why is it sometimes difficult to figure out what God is up to? What can you do the next time you're in a spot when you can't see God's hands?

2. Can you think of another kingdom woman, perhaps more seasoned than you, who has the ability to trust God before the rainbow appears? What can you learn from her?

Prayer

God, I don't always understand what You're up to. When I look at my life, I see only dust. God, give me vision to recognize the rainbow You are creating and faith to trust You when I can't. Amen.

9

Fearing God

Fearing God . . . is a sacred awe
of God's utter holiness.

—John MacArthur, *Successful Christian Parenting*

Ask a roomful of Christian women how they measure up to the superhero of all women of faith—Miss Proverbs 31—and you're sure to see some of them rolling their eyes. No other Bible reference describing something so beautifully big—the character of the godly woman—can make us feel so small! But the voice that whispers our inadequacy, that says we have to accomplish it *all at once*—buying fields, putting dinner on the table, and opening our hands to the poor—is *not* the voice of God. The Lord doesn't ask us to don cape, mask, and lasso to respond to His call in superhuman ways. The kingdom woman isn't a superhero.

She is, however, a woman who fears God. Her understanding of who she is and who God is shapes her priorities. She understands what is hers and what is God's, and that keeps her from becoming overwhelmed. In her season of life, she is faithful to what God has given her.

Application

1. When you read Proverbs 31, do you recognize any qualities of the godly woman that match the season in which you find yourself today? What are they?

2. Can you identify one quality of the Proverbs 31 woman that seems to have your name on it? How will you pursue it?

Prayer

God, help me exhibit the character of the godly woman described in Proverbs 31, the one who fears You. I set my eyes on You today. Amen.

10

People Pleasing

Once you develop a pattern of pleasing people out of fear, it takes a genuine step of faith to break the pattern.

—Joyce Meyer, *Approval Addiction*

Anita had just arrived home from work when the phone rang. Five minutes later, a voice on the other end asked her to coordinate the pastor's appreciation dinner. She wanted to say no. She needed to say no. And yet the word she heard escaping her lips was yes. Though she was already overwhelmed by the demands of work and family, she agreed to coordinate the event.

Too often, like Anita, we care more about pleasing others than about pleasing God. *Might* God have been pleased had Anita said no? Yes! The kingdom woman is someone who *accepts* the assignment that has her name on it and *declines* the one that doesn't. Ill-fitting tasks are to be executed by someone else.

To step toward this freedom by saying no will feel uncomfortable at first for a woman like Anita.

But as she takes that step of faith, she will be set free by seeking her approval from God and not from people.

Application

1. Can you identify some of the kingdom assignments—at work or at church or in your neighborhood—that don't have your name on them and are meant for someone else?

2. Based on who God has called you to be, what types of kingdom-building tasks do you believe God has given you?

Prayer

God, I confess that I've tried to find my worth in pleasing others. Give me the courage to disregard the opinion of others as I seek to please You alone. Amen.

11

God's Voice

Good advertising does not just circulate information. It penetrates the public mind with desires and belief.

—Leo Burnett, pioneer of American advertising

One market research firm estimates that the average American living in a city is exposed to more than five thousand advertisements per day.[1] We *expect* to see ads on billboards and cereal boxes and television commercials, but now ads are being printed on the paper that covers exam tables in pediatricians' offices! We're bombarded with messages meant to shape our behavior—convincing us we *need* a new flat-screen television or the immediate satisfaction of a cool, refreshing soda.

These loud voices penetrate our minds, shaping what we believe and what we want. The kingdom woman, however, tunes her ear to God's voice. Daily she makes choices to turn *down* the volume on the culture's messages about who she is—by closing the revealing fashion magazine or the catalogue or the browser window—so that she might listen for the voice of God. This is the voice by which she is formed, the holy campaign to shape her behavior.

Application

1. To what types of ads—magazine, television, Facebook banners, etc.—are you most susceptible? In what ways do these ads seek to form you and shape your behavior?

2. Through which voices does God speak His true word? Where, in your day, are you tuned in to His true voice?

Prayer

Father, I confess that I am often tempted to find my identity in how the world defines me. Today I will listen for Your voice so that I might be conformed to the image of Jesus. Amen.

12

Spinning Too Many Plates

I'm like one of those circus [performers] spinning plates on sticks. The math tells me that eventually a plate must crash, but I get better and better at the spinning.

—Peter Frankopan, 2012 interview with *Intelligent Life* magazine

Chrystal uses the illustration of a woman spinning too many plates to describe how she felt trying to juggle too many commitments and priorities. Picture a circus clown spinning plates on fingers and toes and even a nose! What Chrystal didn't realize while she was struggling desperately to keep all of her plates spinning, was that other women she admired and respected were—as she was—letting a few crash to the ground. Chrystal began to find relief as she recognized that no one can keep all those plates spinning at once. As she wised up, she realized that while each woman is able to keep some plates spinning, a few ultimately crash. So she learned to prioritize.

The woman who's willing to let go of the spotless home or the pressed slacks can give her attention to what really matters: people.

Chrystal's honesty is a gift to other women. When she allows them to see that some of her plates have crashed to the ground, it frees them up to admit they're not perfect either. When the illusion of being godlike is off the table, women are freed up to be who they really are.

Application

1. What spinning plate or plates has God given you to keep going during this season?

2. What are you trying to juggle right now that God has given you permission to release?

Prayer

God who keeps the planets and galaxies spinning, I confess that I want to be seen as "that woman" who's admired for spinning all the plates. Help me choose the ones that build Your kingdom. Amen.

13

The Most Important Thing

Martha was distracted by her many tasks.

—Luke 10:40, HCSB

Bowls and towels had been set out for the guests' dusty, dirty feet. Cups were being gathered. The table was prepared for a gathering crowd. Food was warming over the fire. Voices were silent, except for one. An honored guest spun stories and offered wise advice, transfixing almost everyone in the house. The name of the lone holdout was Martha.

Martha was Jesus' friend, and an ancient homemaking aficionado, a forerunner to today's Martha Stewart! And even though we know how the story ends, most of us can easily relate to the hostess who was overwhelmed with all that had to be accomplished. The sight of her sister, who was lounging at the Master's feet had Martha seeing red. It wasn't fair! When she finally blew up, Jesus recognized her worry, acknowledged her load, and gently reminded her that Mary had chosen that which, in the moment, was the *most* important thing.

Jesus did, for Martha, exactly what He does for us today. He understands the loads we carry, but He welcomes us to lay them down so we can be with Him.

Application

1. Do you relate to Martha? In what sorts of situations do your responsibilities overwhelm you?

2. If Jesus were to look you in the eye, what would He suggest is the one thing you need to lay down at His feet?

Prayer

God who brings peace, give me the vision to see what is needed most. In the midst of my full day, let me encounter Your face and Your voice. Amen.

14

Hands Open to God

Dear God, I am so afraid to open
my clenched fists!

—Henri Nouwen, *With Open Hands*

One archaeological relic from ancient Greece, a stone carving, depicts two soldiers who are grasping hands. Most experts believe that this gesture, the *handshake*, began as a way for enemies, or strangers, to show that no one was carrying a weapon. Today, more than two thousand years later, this gesture is still used in cultures around the globe. The open hand is a sign of peace.

Our postures, toward others and toward God, might actually be more revealing than we'd like them to be. We keep a good grasp on our purse straps. In unoccupied moments we fiddle with our phones. Some of us hold coffee mugs or diet-soda cans throughout most of the day.

Yet as we reach our open hands toward heaven at the beginning of each day, we're opening ourselves to be used by God as mighty kingdom women.

Application

1. As you move through your day, notice the moments when you're tempted to grab hold of something, or someone, instead of God. What, or whom, do you cling to?

2. In your home or workplace, what sort of gesture—holding out open palms, reaching toward the heavens, etc.—might remind you that God wants to live through you today?

Prayer

God, help me release everything I cling to instead of You. I open my hands to You today. Amen.

15

The Power of Hope

No matter how your heart is grieving / if you keep on believing / the dream that you wish will come true.

—"A Dream Is a Wish Your Heart Makes," *Cinderella*

A lot of women today are living like Cinderella. They are influenced by a wicked stepmother—the devil. He doesn't work alone. He's got two wicked daughters: the world and the flesh. Living as slaves in a hostage situation, many women feel trapped in a hopeless scenario.

Perhaps this describes you in some way. Maybe you even met the Prince of Peace, and He saved you some time ago, but you've found yourself in bondage again. That could mean emotional bondage, spiritual bondage, or even physical bondage.

It's easy to lose heart when you can't see an end. But a kingdom woman clings to hope even in adversity. She cries out like Job, "Though he slay me, I will hope in him" (Job 13:15, ESV).

Cinderella didn't give up. She refused to stay

locked away in the house. She knew a prince was waiting for her. Your Prince is waiting for you, too! Don't give up on the Prince of Peace. He will never give up on you. He's waiting for you to come to the ball.

Application

1. What particular trial or circumstance in your life right now threatens to dampen your hope?

2. How do you cling to the hope you have in the Prince of Peace? Do you pray? Sing? Memorize Scripture?

Prayer

God of hope, shine in my heart. When days are dark, rekindle in me the hope You've promised. Today I turn my eyes from my circumstances and tip them toward You. Amen.

16

God Knows

Please help my people, the poor and downtrod / I thought we all were the children of God / God help the outcasts, children of God!

—"God Help the Outcasts,"

The Hunchback of Notre Dame

Scripture has a lot of stories about people in bondage, who had to wait a long time for freedom or healing. The woman who suffered for eighteen years before Jesus healed her was but one.

When God's people were enslaved in Egypt, Pharaoh forced them to build the cities of Pithom and Rameses. As the Israelites grew in number, and the Egyptians became more fearful of them, their labor was increased. Cruel taskmasters forced them to do everything from working the fields to bricklaying as Pharaoh's massive structures were built. As years, and even centuries, passed, those suffering must surely have wondered if God would *ever* deliver them!

Rather than giving in to the silence of defeat, however, the Israelites lifted their voices to God.

Exodus 2:24–25 says that God *heard* their groaning. God *saw* their suffering. God *remembered* His covenant with Abraham and was concerned. God heard. God saw. God cared. The promise, in the darkness of our own lives, is that the God who delivered the Israelites is the same One in whom we put our trust.

Despite the lies of the enemy, you are not alone. Jesus knows right where you are.

Application

1. In what area(s) of your life have you been most tempted to believe that God abandoned you? Financially? Emotionally? Physically? Spiritually?

2. As you lift your voice to God, you can be certain that He hears, He sees, and He cares. What do you most need to tell God today?

Prayer

God of Israel, I lift my voice to You. Despite the circumstances I face, I trust that You are the God who sees and hears and cares and redeems. Come quickly! Amen.

17

New Clothes

Chosen by God for this new life of love, dress in the wardrobe God picked out for you.

—Colossians 3:12, *The Message*

One of the best parts of Cinderella's story is that the prince never forgot her. Even though a lot of people had been at the ball, something about Cinderella made her stand out from the crowd. She was special. She was unique. She was rare. Everyone wanted the prince, but the prince wanted Cinderella. Perhaps it was Cinderella's clothes.

Her clothes? *But everyone at the ball had nice clothes.*

Cinderella had more than a fancy dress and a tiara. She wore her good character as if it were a cloak. This is how kingdom women are called to live. The apostle Paul affirmed this in Colossians: "You're done with that old life. It's like a filthy set of ill-fitting clothes you've stripped off and put in the fire. Now you're dressed in a new wardrobe" (3:9, MSG). That new wardrobe is the way of life "custom-made by the Creator, with His label on it" (verse 10, MSG). Specifically, we're to be clothed in Christ. Though we're often shortsighted—desiring a new dress from the big-box retailer—God longs to clothe us in the royal garb of Christ himself.

Application

1. Though God longs to give us authentic hope, our desires are often too *small.* How have you been tempted to believe that the next outfit or car or home will bring freedom?

2. If the wardrobe God gives includes compassion, kindness, humility, quiet strength, discipline, and love, which "look" is God offering you today?

Prayer

Giver of all good gifts, I've desired an earthly wardrobe more than I've desired Your wardrobe. Clothe me with Christ today so that I might reflect Your glory. Amen.

18

Made Truly Free

Ah, this is the God I love. . . . The answer to all our fears, Man of Sorrows and Lord of Joy, always permitting what he hates, to accomplish something he loves.

—Joni Eareckson Tada, *The God I Love*

Joni Eareckson Tada had been an active teenager who loved riding horses, playing tennis, and swimming. At seventeen, however, she dove into shallow water in Maryland's Chesapeake Bay, suffering a fracture to her spine. Suddenly paralyzed from the shoulders down, Joni suffered emotionally and even questioned her faith in God. Those familiar with Joni's powerful ministry know that she emerged from the depths of despair as a powerful woman of God, sharing the hope she has in Him through books, radio, and an international ministry among those with disabilities.[1]

Joni may know as well as anyone what it is to be *physically* stuck. But she has chosen to look for hope and a brighter tomorrow. Joni's body may be bound to a wheelchair, but her emotions and spirit are free in Christ. She isn't settling for just getting by. Being a kingdom woman is about connecting with the One who gives hope. A key aspect of the kingdom woman's life is how you view and respond to Jesus.

Joni has—like the bent woman in Luke 13—looked into the face of Jesus and found freedom. Joni's life is a beautiful witness for kingdom women who feel stuck, bound by any variety of frustrations or circumstances or limitations. The kingdom woman who encounters Jesus is set free.

Application

1. Right now, in what ways do you find yourself stuck? Are there ways in which you're bound and are not experiencing freedom?

2. Quiet your heart and listen for Jesus' voice saying to you, "Woman, you are set free." How can you experience that freedom despite your circumstances?

Prayer

God who redeems, I feel as though I've been stuck for so long. Some days I've lost hope and lost sight of You. Today You are the One in whom I find hope. Amen.

19

Responding to God

I was glad when they said unto me,
Let us go into the house of the Lord.

—Psalm 122:1, KJV

Perhaps the most striking invitation was the one Jesus extended to a woman bent over, crippled by disease. Yes, He could have moved toward her as He did toward a paralytic waiting to be dipped into healing waters (John 5:1–9). But instead, He invited her to use the feeble strength she had to move toward Him.

Here Jesus was like a parent who empowers a child by inviting her to do what she is *able* to do for herself. In moving toward Him, toward the good God had for her, He invites this woman to participate in the healing process.

Jesus invited people to be near Him, to leave where they were standing and move in His direction. At the Galilean shore, Jesus invited four common fishermen: "Follow me" (Mark 1:17). Jesus welcomed a despised tax collector named Levi, waiting in his tax booth like a drug dealer who extorts resources from his community. Jesus told Levi, "Follow me" (2:14).

We, too, are invited to actively move toward Jesus. Some of us have the strength to run into Jesus' arms. Others of us, weary and worn, have the energy only to turn our eyes in His direction. Our active response to His invitation is what Jesus is after.

Application

1. As you think about your life during this season, do you feel as if you're moving toward Jesus, standing still, or drifting further from Him?

2. Today Jesus is inviting you to come closer to Him. In what practical way will you respond?

Prayer

Jesus, just as You called Your earliest followers, I hear Your gentle voice today, saying, "Follow Me." Thank You, Lord. And here I come! Amen.

20

Called by Name

The best thing that I can tell you to do if you are facing hopelessness is to listen to Jesus. Hear Him call your name. Like the woman who couldn't straighten up, don't quit.

—Tony Evans, *Kingdom Woman*

Fans crowded into stadium bleachers were going wild. The high school basketball game was tied, and there were only fourteen seconds left on the clock. If the home team could sink just one more basket and keep their crosstown rivals from scoring, the varsity girls team would end their season undefeated. With eight seconds left, the home team's star player was fouled while shooting. As she stepped to the free throw line, she heard the crowd begin to chant. It wasn't wild, as it had been in the heat of the game. In fact, it was a pulsing whisper. *The crowd was saying her name.*

Knees bent and eyes ahead, the girl pounded the ball on the ground twice to center herself; then her whole body uncoiled as she thrust the ball toward the basket. *Swish*! The crowd went wild. Then she did it again. And one minute later, fans burst onto the court still screaming her name. While they'd been cheering for the team most of the game, nothing compared to hearing the sound of her name at the end.

Beloved, this is how Jesus addresses us. He doesn't holler, "Baptists!" or "Methodists!" Rather He calls, "Zacchaeus!" He grins and says, "Mary!" He hasn't called your family or your congregation. Jesus has called *you* by name.

Application

1. When you first came to know Jesus, was it because your family or your faith community had nurtured you into the faith?

2. In what ways has Jesus personally called you?

Prayer

Jesus, quiet all the loud voices that flood my heart and mind. Give me ears to hear the gentle sound of Your voice. Speak, Lord, Your servant is listening. Amen.

21

Daughter of the King

Those of us who have received Christ
are literally children of royalty.
—Beth Moore, *Breaking Free*

One day a princess went hunting in the woods. When she returned, she was almost unrecognizable. The hair under her hood was tousled. Her clothes were torn. Her shoes were caked in mud. Her face was dirty. And she even smelled a little bit. After returning her horse to the stable, she approached the gates of the castle. Curtly, the royal guards turned her away. Pulling off her hood and standing a little straighter, she insisted, "It is I!"

Recognizing her as the princess, the guards bowed and granted her entrance.

Though royal privilege may feel foreign to many of us, it is, nonetheless, our inheritance in Christ! The woman who had suffered for eighteen years was a daughter of Abraham, and Jesus honored her birthright (Luke 13:16). As a kingdom woman, she could capture the ear and heart of God.

In his letter to the Galatians, Paul wrote, "If you are Christ's, then you are Abraham's offspring, heirs according to promise" (3:29, ESV). The promise God made to Abraham—of covenant fidelity and blessing—is the same promise God makes to you. Even if this season of life has been hard for you, your face is dirty, and your hair is mussed, your right to claim your status as God's daughter isn't revocable. You are God's beloved. Proudly enter His kingdom!

Application

1. Does the royal robe of a princess, the rightful garb of a daughter of the King, feel as though it fits you, or does it feel more like the costume of a poser? Why?

2. If you truly see yourself as a royal heir, how will that change the way you move through your day today?

Prayer

King of Kings, too often I forget that I belong to You. Today I choose to live in the reality that I am rightfully Yours. Amen.

22

Love God, Love Excellence

Do you know that nothing you do in this life will ever matter, unless it is about loving God?

—Francis Chan, *Crazy Love*

Even though we want excellence in the things we receive, such as great service in a restaurant, we often lack excellence in the things we do. Yet a kingdom woman understands that her unique position calls her to a high standard. She knows that God has ordained her for a destiny of excellence. But what should motivate a kingdom woman toward excellence?

Imagine that day in and day out, a mother asked her child to help with chores. She reminded him to pick up his dirty socks or load the dishwasher. One day, wanting to wriggle out of his responsibilities, the boy asked, "So what's the one most important thing I'm supposed to do?" The wily boy figured that if he could get his mother to name just one thing, he'd be off the hook for the others!

The Pharisees, like the little boy, tried to trap Jesus in this same way by asking, "Which is the great commandment in the Law?" (Matthew 22:36, ESV). No matter which commandment Jesus chose, they'd be able to nail Him for neglecting another.

His answer, however, silenced them: "You shall love the Lord your God with all your heart and with all your soul and with all your mind" (verse 37, ESV). *Everything*, Jesus emphasized, depends on it.

What this means today is that you were made to love God. In the kingdom woman's home, neighborhood, workplace, church, school, and community, she strives for excellence for the love of God. Love for God is, above all, the thing that matters.

Application

1. When you wake up in the morning, there may be lots of things you don't want to do with excellence. How can focusing on Matthew 22:37 help you set new priorities?

2. Can you name two people whom God has given you during this season that you've been called to love with excellence? Pray for each of them throughout this day.

Prayer

God, I commit myself to loving You and loving others with all my heart, soul, and mind. Amen.

23

Excellence

I do the very best I know how, the very best I can, and I mean to keep on doing so until the end.

—Abraham Lincoln

There are countless Christian women who would love to be married and aren't. There are also plenty of *married* women who have days when they'd rather not be married! One woman is overwhelmed by the demands of her high-powered job as another searches, desperately, for employment.

Excellence isn't concerned with how you are compared to how others are. Excellence is concerned with how you are compared to the potential of how you are supposed to be. In other words, excellence has to do with God's destiny for you. Are you progressively pressing forward and moving toward what He wants for you? Are you defining your decisions, thoughts, and actions by the highest quality and authenticity you have to offer? That is the measure of true excellence.

At one time or another, all of us have wanted our situations to be *other* than they are. In the end, though, the King won't ask us if we got everything we wanted. He will, however, survey what we did with what we were given. If that "something" is singleness, did we maximize the opportunities we had to love and serve? If we've had the opportunity to practice medicine, did we apply ourselves to be the best we could be? If we swept streets, did we do it with as much care as Bach did when composing music? God invites each of us to pursue excellence in the roles we've been given.

Application

1. What is the stuff of your average day? Is your heart burning to be doing something different?

2. How can you practice excellence today in the work you've been given to do?

Prayer

God, I confess that I get restless. I long to do something other than what You've given me. Today, give me passion to serve You with excellence. Amen.

24

SUCCESS

The good you do today, will often be forgotten. Do good anyway. Give the best you have, and it will never be enough. Give your best anyway.

—quote on Mother Teresa's bedroom wall[1]

She wasn't attractive by the world's standards. She was poor. She worked among the dying. She had no husband or children. And yet she was known to millions as "Mother." (Her nickname was Mama T!) The Albanian Roman Catholic nun, Mother Teresa, gave herself to those on the lowest rung of society's ladder. Were it not for the worldwide renown she garnered, which included winning the Nobel Peace Prize in 1979, few looking at this small woman, who led a small life, would have considered her a "success."

By the world's standards, the successful are wealthy. They are powerful. They are attractive. If they "help" people—by providing education or opportunities—then those they help become "successful" as well.

While success belongs to a few, excellence is

available to all. In *God's eyes*, a successful woman fulfills the destiny God has assigned to her. In God's eyes, success doesn't look like the prestigious corner office on the top floor of a skyscraper. Godly success looks like caring for neighborhood children with energy, imagination, and love. True success—excellent living—is when a woman's thoughts, decisions, and actions honor God.

Application

1. In your family of origin, what types of people were considered "successful"?

2. Are you a success in the eyes of the world? What does Christ see when He looks at you? In what ways is God calling you to "success" as a kingdom woman?

Prayer

Mighty God, You are the Potter and I am the clay. Help me to be exactly what You've made me to be and teach me to seek success in Your eyes! Amen.

25

Excellence Doesn't Mean Perfection

It's not about finding ways to avoid God's judgment and feeling like a failure if you don't do everything perfectly. . . . It's about becoming who you really are.

—Stormie Omartian, *The Power of a Praying Woman*

When a parent sees a child struggling over a math problem or working to read an advanced-level book, the parent recognizes that the child isn't yet all that he or she will be. No parent in her right mind would expect a developing child to calculate or read *perfectly*. Instead, the parent is delighted to see her child working to become the person he or she was meant to be. When that child brings home a B or a C on a report card, the parent places the grade in the larger context of the child's attitude and effort, ability and growth.

Somehow, though, it's often harder for us to extend this same kind of grace to ourselves. When we fall short of perfection, we even assume that God's face *frowns* on us. Thankfully, God's standards for us are different from the ones we have for ourselves. Aiming for excellence is different from aiming for perfection. God is more interested in our *becoming who we really are* than in perfection.

Application

1. In which area of your life, if any, do you tend to strive for perfection?

2. What does it look like, for you, to strive for excellence and release the need for perfection?

Prayer

God, I long to become the woman You created me to be. Recognizing that You have more grace for me than I have for myself, help release me from the trap of perfection as I strive toward excellence. Amen.

26

Letting Go of Yesterday

Today's opportunities erase yesterday's failures.

—Gene Brown

Around the country are houses for rehabilitation, also called "halfway houses," where men and women who have fallen on hard times—incarceration, addiction, mental illness—have the opportunity to get a fresh start. In these homes they learn, some for the first time, the skills that will help them function well as they reenter society—filling out a job application, opening a bank account, shopping for groceries on a budget, and so forth. Every day these men and women face a choice: They can look backward, allowing their past to determine their identity, or they can imagine a brighter future for themselves. Which ones succeed? Which ones realize the destiny God has planned for them?

Those of us facing obstacles of our own have the same choice and challenge every day. Like the Bible character Ruth, we can choose to let go of the past and start the future in a new land (Ruth 1:16). Ruth was a woman of excellence because she wasn't held hostage to her past. We can learn from yesterday, but we aren't to live in it.

The devil would love for us to stay stuck in the past. He wouldn't even mind if, dreaming of an unrealistic future, we slacked off on what God has for us today. Each day we have the choice to embrace the future God has prepared for us.

Application

1. How have you been tempted to allow an experience from the past, or a difficult season in your life, define who you are?

2. Living in the past or in the future means we're not really living in the present at all. How can a clear vision of the future impact your living today?

Prayer

God, I believe Your mercies are new every morning. I release yesterday to You, and I purpose to live today as the kingdom woman You've made me to be. Amen.

27

Pleasing People or Pleasing God?

Make sure you are doing what God wants you to do—then do it with all your strength.

—Attributed to George Washington

One problem that often stands in the way of a life of excellence comes when we live for people more than for God. We make people our standard rather than God. We do our jobs for those around us, we work for our family's praise, we make our actions and choices in light of how people are going to respond to us rather than whether God is going to say that we are excellent.

For example, we all have known a "Stacey," someone who appeared to be the very model of a kingdom woman. Stacey was committed to serving in her church and in the community. She pursued excellence in all she did. Her house appeared effortlessly clean. Her children were well behaved. So what was the problem? It was her motivation.

Stacey *performed* for the eyes of others. She

didn't sneak into church to organize the Sunday school closets without making sure someone knew what she was up to. After serving at the homeless shelter, she'd mention it in conversation. Fearful of being judged by others, she angrily forced her children to clean up the house and themselves before company arrived at the door. Stacey's choices and actions were determined by what others thought of her, not by God's standard of excellence.

The kingdom woman, though, wants most to please God. Striving to be excellent in God's eyes is what motivates her. Yes, it may mean that she won't always shine in the eyes of others, but her passion is to catch the eye of her God.

Application

1. You probably know someone like Stacey. More important, do you recognize any of her in yourself?

2. What one thing can you do this week for the eyes of God alone?

Prayer

God, I recognize my own temptation to appear acceptable to others. Forgive me. Teach me to disregard the opinion of others and seek Your approval instead. Amen.

28

Known for Excellence

Excellence is to do a common thing in an uncommon way.

—Booker T. Washington, African-American educator

Imagine you're at the movies with a friend, and you run into an acquaintance you know from work. The three of you chat a bit, and then the acquaintance moves on. After she leaves, you might remark to your friend, "She's a special woman. She's so very thoughtful." Or you might complain, "She's a tough one! Most of us have a hard time getting along with her." Or you might even say, "I'm so impressed by her. She's committed to caring for a brother who's mentally ill." What *identifies* this woman, in your mind, is what stands out about her character.

A kingdom woman is known to others, and commended, as a woman of excellence. Like Phoebe, whom the apostle Paul commended for being a servant of the church and a help to many (Romans 16:1–2), the kingdom woman is known, recognized, and identified by her excellence of character. Whether she's organizing a church supper or teaching Sunday school or taking out the garbage, others notice her.

Application

1. Are you someone who notices and commends excellence in others?

2. In which area of your life could you grow in excellence?

Prayer

God, I want to be known—to others, but mostly to You!—as a woman of excellence. Teach me to walk in Your ways so that I bring glory to Your name. Amen.

29

Excellence in the Quiet Place

It is Christianity to be gentle, merciful and forgiving, and to keep those qualities quiet in our own hearts, and never make a boast of them, or of our prayers or of our love of God.

—Charles Dickens, *The Life of Our Lord*

When athletes or pop stars or comedians perform at Madison Square Garden, it's because they're known for excellence. They've honed their skills for years, and on the night of the championship game or big show, they focus on giving an excellent performance for those gathered. That they give their very best in front of thousands isn't particularly commendable. It's just *expected.*

What's *commendable* is striving for excellence in *secret.* It's the NBA player going home and washing the dirty dishes. It's the rock idol shoveling a neighbor's driveway while she's at work. It's the popular comedian pausing to set up chairs and tables at church. When Jesus described how His followers are to give and to pray and to fast,

He advised them to practice it all with a low profile. They are to perform for the eyes of the Father, "who sees what is done in secret" (Matthew 6:18).

Application

1. In what ways do you strive for excellence that is public in nature?

2. This week, how will you fast, pray, or serve in a way that goes entirely unnoticed by others?

Prayer

God, I confess that I like for my good works to be seen by others. Give me a heart that longs to please only You and teach me to practice righteousness in the secret places. Amen.

30

On That Day

God will help you if you'll help
yourself by giving your best.
—Ben Carson, *Think Big*

An archer raises the taut bow she holds in her left hand and positions an arrow with her right. As she draws back her right arm, her eye is fixed on the target ahead. With machinelike precision, her entire body is aligned toward the target. When the bowstring has reached optimal tension, her fingers release, and the arrow flies toward its mark. The smallest flinch or misalignment will send the arrow hurtling away from its goal. When she's accurate, however, the arrow sinks into the center of the red-and-white bull's-eye with a satisfying *thunk*!

Chrystal's auntie, whom she describes as a woman of excellence, has the vision of an archer. When asked what motivates her, this woman of God replies, "Because of that day." "That day" is Auntie's reference to the day she expects to stand before Jesus, and He tests the quality of her work.

The truth is that we all will face "that day," and if the service we've offered Him is excellent, we'll hear those blessed words, "Well done, good and faithful servant. . . . Enter into the joy of your master" (Matthew 25:23, ESV).

When a kingdom woman's eyes are set on that target, every part of her body aligns toward a single goal. Her eyes are tipped toward the bull's-eye that Auntie calls "that day."

Application

1. What woman do you know who exemplifies a life of excellence? What does that look like?

2. What would be different this week if you set your eyes on "that day"?

Prayer

God, help me keep my eyes on the target You've set before me. Teach me to be single-hearted, focused on You and who You've called me to be. Amen.

31

Commitment in the Dark

We are closest to God in the darkness,
stumbling along blindly.

—Madeleine L'Engle, *Two-Part Invention*

Today women who are pregnant can pay top dollar to sneak a peek at the baby in their womb by getting a 3-D ultrasound. During most of a woman's pregnancy, a doctor can monitor the fetus's growth. Specialists now even perform surgery on unborn babies. Advances in science and technology have shined a light on what happens in the darkness of the womb.

A few thousand years ago, however, parents were as much in the dark as their developing babies were! Without access to ultrasound medical procedures, parents had to trust what God was up to in the dark. At first it seemed as though nothing was growing inside at all. Then a bulging belly would show what God had been up to.

Even though we can't see God working, that doesn't mean He's idle. God does some of His best work in the dark. He does some of His best work when we don't think He's doing a thing. He's behind the scenes, working it out. He is faithful even though we can't see Him.

If it feels as if the darkness is closing in, don't despair. God is not absent. In the darkness we wait in *trust* for God's light to shine.

Application

1. It's easiest to trust God in the light. In what seasons of your life has it been most easy to trust Him?

2. In what season was it most difficult for you to trust God?

3. On what do you rely when God seems far away? What brings you comfort?

Prayer

God, confident You do Your best work in the dark, I trust what my eyes cannot see. I believe that You are at work in the darkness, and I wait for Your light to shine. Amen.

32

Depending on God

The end of ourselves is always
a new beginning in God.
—Dorothy Womack, *How to Lay*
on the Altar Without Wiggling

The woman in 2 Kings 4 went to Elisha, a prophet of God, because she was in a situation that only God could fix. Have you ever been in a situation that only God can fix? You've tried everything you can think of to fix it, but nothing has worked.

If you are in or have been in a situation like that, it's most likely that God has you exactly where He wants you. Sometimes God lets you be in a situation that only He can fix, so you'll discover that He is the One who can fix it. You'll never discover that God is all you need until you get to the place where God is all you have.

When your abilities to make things work have been depleted, you are in a situation that is beyond your own resources, and even beyond the resources of those around you. When the bank won't give you a loan, when your friends won't answer the phone, when the doctors can't pinpoint what's ailing you, you are beyond your own resources. When you've talked to every person you can think of, and no one intervenes on your behalf, you realize that God is all you have. That's where this woman in the Bible was, so she went straight to the prophet.

Application

1. Have you ever been among Christian people without resources, who were full of faith and joy—perhaps on a missions trip overseas? What did you notice?

2. Sometimes faith comes precisely when we're out of resources. When have you been in a desperate situation where you could only trust in God?

Prayer

God, when my situation is beyond my own resources and beyond the resources of those around me, I can always trust You. Today I won't depend on my own abilities. Today You are all I have. Amen.

33

A Word Just for You

Speak, for your servant is listening.

—1 Samuel 3:10

In Scripture, God communicates in different ways. A *logos* is a general word of what He says.[1] Yet a *rhema* is a specific utterance with a specific situation or person in mind.[2]

Former pro-baseball pitcher Frank Pastore and his wife, Gina, received a *rhema* more than two decades ago. Gina recalls,

> We were on staff with Campus Crusade at the time, and Frank had a desire to attend graduate school. Was it law school or was it seminary? We kept praying about this choice. One day out of the blue, we received a call from a friend we hadn't spoken with in a long time. He shared, "The Lord gave me a dream . . . I don't know what this means, but, He told me to share it with you. Does 'Go to Seminary' mean anything to you?" Frank and I were blown away and just

stared at each other. The message was so extraordinary that we simply obeyed. Frank went to seminary.

Frank's seminary degree played a key role in his ministry to millions. For nine years Frank hosted a dynamic Christian drive-time talk show for KKLA radio station in Los Angeles: *The Frank Pastore Show*.[3]

The woman who cried out to Elisha for help received a special message from the prophet (2 Kings 4:3). Because the widow committed herself to the instructions of the message, she experienced a miracle. Kingdom women obey God's Word even when it seems to make no sense. Faith doesn't always make sense, but it does make miracles.

Application

1. God speaks most clearly through Scripture. When, if ever, have you heard God speaking *to you* through the Bible? A particular verse?

2. How has God spoken directly to you? Through a sermon? A Bible verse? A friend? Did you act on that message? Why or why not?

Prayer

God, You are faithful. I thank You that You speak through Your Word and Your people. Give me ears to hear Your voice today. Speak, Lord, Your servant is listening. Amen.

34

The Seasoned Woman

Generally, by the time you are Real, most of your hair has been loved off, and your eyes drop out and you get loose in the joints and very shabby.

—Margery Williams, *The Velveteen Rabbit*

Recently a celebrity's online blog offered a list of things that get better with age. On that list was cast-iron skillet, blue jeans, love letters, and baseball mitts. Like the old story of the velveteen rabbit, the stuffed toy whose fur got loved off, some things get better the more they're worn and read and used.

We tend to look at people who have life wounds and wonder what has happened to them. Sometimes those battle scars are a result of struggles that person brought on herself. Sometimes that person may have had no fault at all in the acquisition of her injuries. From the outside looking in, we may stop and stare because we tend to dislike noticeable imperfections. The fact of the matter is that many women with scuff marks are simply seasoned and, therefore, more available for God's use because of their imperfection, inadequacy, or emptiness.

The kingdom woman who has experienced injury or hardship isn't *less* prepared to serve; she is *more* prepared. Seasoned—like that old cast-iron skillet—her imperfections allow her to connect with others.

Application

1. In your family, church, or community, whom do you consider *wise*? Has this person had his or her share of life's troubles?

2. Consider some of the giants of the faith: Moses and Joseph in the Old Testament, Peter and Paul in the New. How were they scuffed and stained by life?

Prayer

God, I confess that in my flesh, I would rather avoid life's troubles, trials, and tribulations. Because that's not possible, use all I've faced to season me as a useful instrument in Your hands. Amen.

35

World Values, Kingdom Values

Rather than love, than money,
than fame, give me truth.
—Henry David Thoreau, *Walden*

One of the biggest challenges in our Christian experience is committing to follow God's wisdom rather than the world's. The world's wisdom is sometimes referred to as worldliness. Worldliness is simply that system set up by Satan that seeks to leave God out.

In our culture, there's no bigger gap between godliness and worldliness than in appearance. If you were to ask a room full of women how the world values women's bodies, you'd hear this: a trim figure, smooth skin, good hair, perfect features.

If you asked how *God* values women's bodies, that might be harder to answer. God wants women to take care of their bodies. He wants His followers to be healthy. God values modesty. Kingdom values aren't nearly as glamorous as Hollywood's!

This is the message of Scripture. Again and again, God takes the world's values and turns them upside down. Though the world values pride, privilege, fame, and physical beauty, God values humility, emptiness, meekness, and the beauty of a servant's heart. The kingdom woman chooses to embrace the values God esteems.

Application

1. What does God see when He looks at your body? Does He see bones and muscles that serve others?

2. The influence of the world on our thinking is powerful. How are you tempted to value what the world values?

3. Today, how will you choose to embrace God's values?

Prayer

God, I thank You that You don't value what the world values. Father, I desire Your purposes more than I value a life of ease. Empower me today to choose what pleases You. Amen.

36

The Humble Person

Do not imagine that if you meet a really humble man he will be what most people call "humble" nowadays. . . . Probably all you will think about him is that he seemed a cheerful, intelligent chap who took a real interest in what you said to him. . . . He will not be thinking about humility: he will not be thinking about himself at all.

—C. S. Lewis, *Mere Christianity*

Have you ever been around someone who takes a real interest in you? This person makes you feel special, though you have no outstanding merits. It might be a teacher or a coach. It might be the parent of a friend or someone at church. In the presence of this person, you feel as though you're really seen and heard and known.

As C. S. Lewis said, taking a genuine interest in others, without thinking about oneself at all, is the mark of true humility.[1] This humble person doesn't go on and on about having a bad hair day. She doesn't draw attention to her achievements and accomplishments. She might not talk about herself at all. What will be true of her is that she takes a real interest in who *you* are.

There is no such thing as a proud kingdom woman, because the terms are mutually exclusive. The pursuit of humility isn't a matter of convincing ourselves that we are *nothing*. Rather, it's a powerful confidence that because we are *somebody*, we have been set free from self-absorption to turn our attention to others. The woman of humility is the one who, without thought for herself, gives herself freely to others.

Application

1. Think of a woman in your life who notices others—their concerns, gifts, problems, etc.—rather than being absorbed with herself.

2. As you seek to grow in humility, in what areas of your life might God be inviting you to think of yourself less? How might this free you to give to others?

Prayer

God, because I'm confident in You and who You have made me to be, I'm set free from being preoccupied with myself. Give me a vision to see others as You see them. Amen.

37

WOMAN OF SACRIFICE

My job was to simply follow His leading one step at a time, holding every decision up to Him in prayer.

—Corrie ten Boom, *The Hiding Place*

Corrie ten Boom was a Dutch Christian who, with her family, helped Jews in Holland escape the Holocaust during World War II. The daughter of Christians, Corrie had been raised from a young age to trust in God's provision. In 1944 her family was arrested. Corrie and her sister, Betsie, were sent to a concentration camp in Germany, where Betsie died. After the war, Corrie continued to help Holocaust survivors in the Netherlands.

A kingdom woman, Corrie valued God's plan for her more than an easy life. She was willing to jeopardize her life so that God might use her to help save Jewish lives. With little power of her own, she chose instead to be filled with God's love and power.

Today the kingdom woman seeks not her own happiness but to be used by God.

Application

1. What securities and privileges did Corrie ten Boom sacrifice to be used by God?

2. What privileges do you enjoy that might keep you from being used by God?

3. In what area of your life, if any, has God asked you to make sacrifices so that He might use you?

Prayer

God, I trust You, and I'm willing to be used by You. Today I release the plans I have for myself and choose the plans You have for me. Amen.

38

A Little Bit

If you believe, you will receive whatever you ask for in prayer.

—Matthew 21:22

In baking, some ingredients are scooped out in large measure. Dough uses cupfuls of flour. Sweet baked goods require lots of sugar. But other ingredients are portioned out in small measure. Cookies don't need more than a teaspoon of vanilla. Cakes don't need cups of baking powder. Bread needs the smallest amount of yeast.

When God asks us to exercise our faith, He doesn't demand that we have a five-pound sack of it. Sometimes believers will, but more often, God asks for a little bit of faith. In fact, Jesus said that it doesn't have to be any bigger than a tiny mustard seed! (See Matthew 17:20.)

In your circumstances today, are you struggling to have *big* faith? Does it appear that the recipe to solve your problems requires an unusually large amount of faith? Approaching your situation that way makes you the solution to your problems! But God asks only for your small offering of faith. Then He takes that little dash of faith and does big things with it!

Application

1. What are some powerful ingredients that require only a tiny portion to be effective (such as a spark!)?

2. Do you consider yourself a person of big faith, little faith, or somewhere in between? Today, how will you give God your offering of little faith?

Prayer

God, as the children's song says, "[We] are weak, but He is strong"! Take the faith I offer in weakness and multiply it with Your strength, for Your glory. Amen.

39
How You Are Defined

Define yourself radically as one
beloved by God. This is the true self.
Every other identity is illusion.

—Brennan Manning, *Abba's Child*

When people meet one another at social events, the first thing they do is to exchange names. Next, they usually ask, "What do you do?" People want to know what others do to identify them. One woman might answer, "I'm a stay-at-home mother and homeschool my four children." Another woman might say, "I'm a professor and teach at the university." Yet another woman might say, "I'm retired." First and foremost, the world defines us by what we *do*.

The kingdom woman doesn't define herself by what she does. Ultimately, she doesn't even find her identity in her relationships—as daughter, sister, wife, mother. The kingdom woman is *defined* by her relationship to God. First and foremost, God defines her by *who she is*. Who she is, says God, is *beloved* (Romans 9:25; 11:28).

Whether the kingdom woman is raising children, raising test scores, or raising prayers, the foundation of her identity is that she is loved by God.

Application

1. When you meet someone for the first time, how do you describe what you do with your time?

2. Imagine meeting a new friend and introducing yourself by sharing your name and the fact that you are deeply loved. How does the rest of that conversation go?

Prayer

God, I thank You that Your love defines who I am. Though the world defines me otherwise, teach me to live in the reality of who I am in You: beloved. Amen.

40

A Woman of Powerful Faith

PRAY, v. To ask that the laws of the universe be annulled in behalf of a single petitioner confessedly unworthy.

—*The Devil's Dictionary of Ambrose Bierce*

A gospel crusade in South Carolina had brought together twenty-five thousand people to hear the Word of God. But dark, tall storm clouds had gathered above the stadium. The organizers feared the event would have to be cancelled due to rain.

The pastors and leaders gathered together in a small room. They prayed and asked God to stop the rain. A petite woman named Linda gave the closing request: "Lord, we told these people that if they would come out tonight they would hear a word from God. . . . Therefore right now I ask in the Name of the Lord Jesus Christ for the rain to stop for the sake of Your Name!"

Soon the rain rushed toward the stadium like a wall of water. Yet when it hit the stadium, it split. Half of the rain went on one side of the stadium. The other half went on the other side.

Then it literally met on the other side of the stadium.

When people learn that God answered Linda's bold prayer to stop the rain so that people could hear the Word of God, they begin to wonder if that kind of relationship with God is possible for them. Linda didn't save her prayer to be prayed in front of others. Linda had developed an intimacy with God. She and God had built a very unique relationship. She trusted that God was good. She was fearless in her prayer. The relationship Linda had with God is available to you. As you pray, remember Linda's boldness. Let it give you permission to go deeper with God.

Application

1. When others pray with great boldness, how does that make you feel?

2. Do you pray with this type of boldness? Do you know someone who does?

3. How would your prayers be different if you truly believed that God's name was at stake?

Prayer

God, You are the One who moves mountains. You say that we can do it too. Teach me to trust in the power of Your name so that I might learn to pray with mountain-moving faith. Amen.

41

Releasing Control

So, let us humble ourselves under the hand of God in every trial and trouble, for He will save and raise up the humble in spirit.

—Thomas à Kempis, *The Inner Life*

Don't you love sports? Most sports demand intense focus and concentration. Gifted athletes work tirelessly for years to hone their skills. The golf swing of Tiger Woods, the backhand of Venus or Serena Williams, or the precision of *any* Dallas Cowboy quarterback is a thing of beauty. These athletes have learned how to control their bodies and their tools with precision. With bent knees and an open stance, they've trained themselves to respond with agility and control.

Many of us can be tempted to live our lives this way. We improve and excel in our jobs. We implement effective strategies to manage our homes or our families. We even develop effective habits of prayer and meditation. The temptation, however, is that we'll begin to believe the subtle lie that *we are in control.*

The woman who had been subject to bleeding for twelve long years and humbly crawled on her knees to Jesus had no illusion that she was in control. For twelve years, no one had been able to heal her. There was no swing or pass or technique she could master to preserve the illusion she was in control of her life.

Though most of us wouldn't willingly *choose* such a lack of control, such vulnerability, the humble posture of kneeling uniquely positions us to receive what Jesus has to offer. Will you choose to adopt it?

A kingdom woman is a woman who knows and believes that her solution is not found in money, human reasoning, or other people. Her solution is found in humbling herself before Jesus Christ and surrendering to the Word of God.

Application

1. In what area of your life would it be most difficult to give up control? Do you hear God's voice inviting you to do it?

2. This week, how will you carve out time and space to bow before God and release control to Him?

Prayer

God, I confess that I feel most secure when I'm able to control my life—my finances, my work, my family, and my life. Teach me to release control to You. Amen.

42

Holy Deal Making

Lord Almighty, if you will only look on your servant's misery and remember me, and not forget your servant but give her a son, then I will give him to the Lord for all the days of his life, and no razor will ever be used on his head.

—1 Samuel 1:11

On the television game show *Let's Make a Deal* that began in the 1960s, contestants wagered varying amounts of money with energetic host Monty Hall. The announcer would ask something like, "Would you make a deal to trade five hundred dollars in cash for one of these three doors, knowing behind one of them is $4,729 in cash or valuable merchandise?" The contestant would decide whether to deal or keep the cash. Depending on their luck, contestants would sometimes lose it all, and sometimes they would clean up big.

We make deals in life all the time. We may make a deal with a friend to take her to a movie if she loses ten pounds. We tell our bosses we'll do extra work for extra pay or a promotion.

We can't make deals with God, however, because God is God. We have no bargaining chip. He already controls us and our circumstances.

But once in a while, God honors a kingdom follower. Hannah offered God a deal in the form of a vow, and He took it. She told God that if He would give her a son, then she would give that same son back to serve Him in the temple all the days of his life. Hannah, a kingdom woman, honored God with her faithful response. When it would have been incredibly tempting to keep Samuel to herself, she released him into God's care and was blessed.

Application

1. How do you react to the idea of making a deal with God? Does it make you uncomfortable?

2. How might Hannah have convinced herself to keep Samuel at home after his birth?

3. Have you ever made a promise like this to God? Did you follow through?

Prayer

God, You are the giver of all good gifts. Though I don't pretend to control You, I do—like Hannah—want to offer you the things I hold most dear. Teach me how to honor You as a kingdom woman. Amen.

43

Unlikely Faith

We must cease striving and trust God to provide what He thinks is best and in whatever time He chooses to make it available. But this kind of trusting doesn't come naturally. It's a spiritual crisis of the will in which we must choose to exercise faith.

—Charles Swindoll, *Jesus, the Greatest Life of All*

One of the most exciting acts to watch when the circus comes to town is the flying trapeze. Talented gymnasts hurtle through the air, *trusting* they'll be caught by a partner on the other side. This sort of courage doesn't come naturally to most of us. Before releasing her grasp on the bar she holds, the performer must *believe* she'll be caught. To let go when there's a safety net positioned below requires some amount of courage. To let go when there's no safety net requires a *lot* of faith!

When Elijah asked the widow of Zarephath for food, she didn't exercise safety-net faith, knowing she had a stockpile of food in the pantry. No, she released her grip on the little she had because she trusted that her life was in the hands of the One who wouldn't let her fall.

In the end, safety-net faith isn't really *faith* at all. Rather, faith happens when we trust God to provide for us when we don't have a back-up plan.

Application

1. When was the last time you trusted God entirely for something you could not yet see?

2. Today, is God asking you to release something so that you can depend entirely on Him? What sort of fears keep you from trusting God to provide in miraculous ways?

Prayer

God, give me the faith of the widow who trusted—beyond what her eyes could see—that You are a faithful Provider. I release what I have to You, because You are good. Amen.

44

A Pattern of Faithfulness

Her actions, thoughts, and decisions leading up to that point had made her a woman who caught God's special attention.

—Tony Evans, *Kingdom Woman*

Some of us at home on couches can picture ourselves running the 400-meter dash during the summer Olympics or dunking the ball in the last few seconds of the WNBA finals. And sometimes we have the same sorts of fantasies about our spiritual lives. We imagine standing up for the name of Christ under persecution or clinging to our faith in the most hopeless circumstances. The real question, though, is whether our current "training" is preparing us for game time.

The folks God chose for some of His really big assignments—people like Noah, Moses, and Mary—hadn't been at home on their couches. They had already demonstrated a willingness to say *yes* to God. They'd already been in training for the jobs God had for them. And some of those assignments were pretty outlandish! God doesn't use believers who just dream of being faithful. Instead, God's eyes search for kingdom women who are in the *habit* of saying yes to Him.

Application

1. Are you in the habit of saying yes to God?

2. What small thing could you do this week to say yes to God? (It could be as simple as committing to a regular prayer time or to sharing your faith with someone at work.)

Prayer

God, develop me into the kind of kingdom woman You would be pleased to use as a builder of Your kingdom. By Your Spirit, help me to establish godly habits as I pattern my life after Jesus. Amen.

45

Built Brick by Brick

The greatest act of faith some days is to simply get up and face another day.

—Amy Gatliff, *The Power to Never Give Up*

Did you play with wooden building blocks or plastic building toys as a child? Some of the things that children—and adults!—can make today with plastic building bricks are absolutely amazing. A quick search on-line will reveal that one creator has replicated the world-famous "Last Supper" painting. Another has modeled a larger-than-life Batman. Another has made a stunning replica of the US Capitol building. Each creation has one thing in common: Each piece was added—by hand, not by machine—brick by brick.

"Brick by brick" is how Chrystal describes her grandmother's faith, formed over a lifetime. This woman who was committed to God's plans and purposes for her life decided to follow God one day at a time. She didn't wake up one morning and suddenly have the kind of faith that moves mountains. Rather, she made daily decisions that formed her as a woman of faith. Thought by thought, word by word, action by action, she pursued God with her whole heart. A true woman of faith, Chrystal's grandmother chose, moment by moment, to believe in the goodness of God.

Application

1. What types of small decisions—the "bricks"—form, one by one, a solid faith? Have you been purposefully placing one brick on top of another in your walk of faith?

2. If you haven't been practicing this brick-by-brick method of faith building, now is the moment to start. What small faith-building decision is God asking of you today?

Prayer

God, when I'm old I want to be the kind of kingdom woman who has built a solid foundation on You, the Rock of my salvation. Give me the strength and endurance to build the kind of faith that endures. Amen.

46

Medicinal Obedience

The natural mind prefers argument to obedience, solutions to truth.

—Elisabeth Elliot, *Discipline: The Glad Surrender*

During Apartheid in South Africa, a period of government-directed segregation, activists were calling on nations including the United States to stop trading with South Africa. The idea was that by ceasing trade, other nations would apply persuasive economic pressure on the South African government to compel a change in its unjust laws. Unfortunately, in situations like these, those hardest hit by the economic restrictions are usually the poor, not the lawmakers. In South Africa, however, many activists among the poor were requesting sanctions. The reason? These advocates for justice were willing to taste the bitter medicine of hardship because they had confidence that in the end, their country would enjoy better health because of it.

When God asks us to follow His instructions, it can often feel like bitter medicine. Some of us may turn to the Word of God and feel good about how wonderful the prescription sounds and all of the things that it's supposed to do, but we stay "sick" because we don't ingest the "medicine" God gives us. Only when we respond in obedience—even when, and maybe especially when it's difficult—do we experience the full benefits of our faith.

Application

1. Is there a situation in your life in which you know God has asked for obedience, and you've been slow to respond?

2. Today, how will you take one step in the direction of obedience?

Prayer

God, I believe that You are the One who can make all things right. Though I've been slow to respond in faithfulness to You, give me courage to obey You today. Amen.

47

Humility

Humility is simply acknowledging the truth of [our] position as creature, and yielding to God His place.

—Andrew Murray, *Humility*

An acquaintance of mine used to visit a facility for people with severe intellectual and physical disabilities. Residents there would get from place to place using wheelchairs or canes. Some had to be carried on stretchers or rolling beds. To keep their muscles and connective tissue from contracting severely, some of the residents would spend time strapped onto "kneelers" or "standers" or would lie on boards that helped extend their ligaments and tendons.

While these folks didn't *choose* to assume humble postures—kneeling or lying prostrate—their very bodies symbolized the truth about who we are before a holy God. When our bodies reflect the reality of our relatedness to God, it's as if we're praying with our posture and our hearts. Some people kneel in prayer. Others, in desperation, lie prostrate before God. Others, more physically limited, may simply lower their eyes to acknowledge the reality and nearness of a holy and mighty God.

A kingdom woman of faith must pursue both Christ and the authority of the Scripture with a heart of humility. If you will humble yourself to grab hold of His Word, His power is yours.

Application

1. What postures do you use when you pray to God? Do you raise your hands in praise? Drop to your knees in prayer? Bow your head?

2. How might you incorporate a posture of humility into your prayer life this week?

Prayer

Lord, I thank You that You are God and I am not. As I bow, kneel, or lie at Your feet, I recognize the reality of Your power and might. Amen.

48

A Spiritual Approach to Unsolvable Problems

The only hope and lasting change that is going to come is going to come through a spiritual solution.

—Greg Laurie, interview with the *Christian Post*, August 23, 2012

If a woman develops a skin condition, a rash, or chronic itching, she'll typically seek help from a dermatologist. If her child struggles in school, she may hire a tutor. When a line of ants parades into her home, she might call an exterminator. She identifies the source of the problem and seeks the help of a professional.

But what if she misidentifies the source of the problem? The dermatologist won't be useful if she continues to use a detergent to which she's allergic. If her child has a learning disability, she might also need to seek medical advice. And if her child is leaving food packages open in the pantry, attracting ants, she needs to teach that child about the consequences.

When we wrongly self-diagnose a problem in our lives, we won't get the help we need to transform it. When a loved one is battling addiction, when a friend suffers from depression, or when a child's behavior is out of line, the kingdom woman asks herself, "Does this problem have a spiritual root?" It doesn't mean she won't consult a specialist, but she prays to and puts her trust in the One who specializes in healing the whole person.

Application

1. Who are the go-to authorities in your life for the kinds of problems you face?

2. What problem do you face, if any, that you suspect might have a spiritual root?

3. How will you pray—and behave!—differently when you approach your problems spiritually?

Prayer

God, too often I see life the way the world sees it. Teach me to view my life the way You see it. Because You are the source of my life, You are also the source of my healing! Amen.

49

Courage

Courage: mental or moral strength to venture, persevere, and withstand danger, fear, or difficulty.

—Merriam-Webster Online Dictionary

On December 1, 1955, Rosa Parks was tired. She'd worked all day and was ready to be home. When seats in the white section of the Montgomery, Alabama, city bus filled up, the bus driver moved the whites-only section marker to include the seat Parks occupied. The driver waved his hand, as if swatting flies, to instruct people of color to give up their seats. Rosa Parks, described as the first lady of the Civil Rights Movement, recalls, "When that white driver stepped back toward us, when he waved his hand and ordered us up and out of our seats, I felt a determination cover my body like a quilt on a winter night."[1] In that moment, Parks was fueled by *courage*.

Courage to persevere despite any fear or danger we might face is what Jesus asks of the kingdom woman. Like Rosa Parks, she may be called to stand up for the cause of justice. Like the woman who was healed by touching the hem of Jesus' garment, she may be called to testify to His goodness. The kingdom woman may be asked to reach out and care for someone Jesus loves who lives in a dangerous place. Depending on the grace Jesus provides, the kingdom woman boldly follows where He leads.

As a kingdom woman, you have been called to support your family, raise your children, and honor your husband, but you have also been called to make a maximum impact for God's kingdom. You aren't to deny the other purposes in your life, but you aren't to limit yourself to them either. A kingdom woman has a destiny that extends beyond her home—the legacy you leave with your community and possibly even your nation and the world.

Application

1. Besides Rosa Parks, what other kingdom women can you think of who have acted courageously?

2. Has Jesus called you to speak up or take action for something you'd rather not? With the courage He provides, how will you respond?

Prayer

God, give me the courage of a Rosa Parks. More than I want worldly security, I want to speak up and take action as You lead. With Your strength, teach me to follow. Amen.

50

Follow, Follow

Follow, follow, follow, follow,
follow the yellow brick road.
—"Follow the Yellow Brick Road," *The Wizard of Oz*

In the acclaimed 1939 motion picture *The Wizard of Oz*, the beloved heroine, Dorothy, joined a single-minded crew of motley characters in their journey to see the Wizard, who would meet the longings of their hearts. More than anything, the Scarecrow wanted a brain, the Tin Man longed for a heart, and the Lion was eager to receive courage. Despite all kinds of obstacles, Dorothy and her friends followed the yellow brick road in their pursuit of the Wizard.[1]

In life, some roads or paths lead us to where we want to go, and some paths lead us away from where we want to end up. Some roads are smooth, some are rocky, some are slippery, and some will get us stuck. I've personally traveled along paths that were painful and paths that brought me so much joy I felt I would burst.

God always asks us to walk the pathway of

faith. Simply put: Choose to walk the path God has placed in front of you. Sometimes, we don't know what our paths hold; in fact, most times we have no idea what our journeys will bring. These are the pathways with a direction and end you cannot see. The way ahead may seem blurry, but just stay on the road, and you'll find your path ultimately leads to Jesus.

Application

1. What path has God set before you? Do you know where the path will end?

2. Is it all right to walk toward God without knowing where your final destination will be? Why or why not?

Prayer

Lord, with my heart and mind, I believe the path toward You is the only road for me. Today, give me the strength and desire to run. Amen.

51

TRUE WORDS

Faith is acting like something is so, even when it is not so, in order that it might be so simply because God said so.

—Tony Evans, *Kingdom Woman*

A mother has just set a delicious dinner on the dining-room table. She calls to her children to wash their hands and come to dinner. One child is busy playing video games. One is watching television. One is doing homework. As she pours water into their glasses, no children arrive at the table. Directing her voice upstairs toward her children, she calmly announces, "If you are not at this table in sixty seconds, hands washed, you will not have screen privileges for one week."

What happens? Well, it depends. If the children don't believe their mother is telling the truth, if they think she won't follow through on her word, they'll continue to tarry. If they believe that what she says is true, those children will race to wash their hands and land in their dinner chairs with seventeen seconds to spare!

If we don't yet believe that what God says is true, we have no reason to move into action. And faith without action isn't really faith at all (James 2:17). However, when we do believe that God's words are true, our bodies will respond. Acting on God's words, before we have the proof that what He says is true, is the stuff of real faith.

The real measure of our relationship with Christ and our faith in Christ is our ability to act based on what we know. It's the ability to stick with it even when we can't see our way.

Application

1. Describe a situation in your life when you acted on God's words, believing that what He speaks is true.

2. Today, how do you sense God asking you to step out in faith?

Prayer

God, I want to be a woman who moves into action at the sound of Your words. Give me faith to see what I cannot yet see and courage to walk in Your ways. Amen.

52

Walk It to Work It

Work the program, and the program will work for you.

—Recovery-community slogan

When addicts and alcoholics finally reach the end of their ropes—when they hurt loved ones, crash vehicles, endanger themselves and others, or get fired—many are finally willing to get help. When these sufferers turn to support groups like Narcotics Anonymous or AA (Alcoholics Anonymous), fellow pilgrims on the journey come alongside them to show them the path to health and wholeness. One of the firm admonitions these veterans offer the rookies is, "Work the program. If you work the program," these seasoned helpers insist, "the program will work for you!"

This is what Chrystal was saying to kingdom women when she wrote, "Choose to walk the path God has placed in front of you, and put one foot in front of the other." Don't waste time thinking, *I know this has worked for other people, but it won't work for me.* Don't second-guess God, reasoning, "I think my way would be a little faster than His way." Even when the way ahead seems unclear, taking one step at a time is what will get you to the destination God has planned. To "work the program" God has designed for your welfare is to walk daily in obedience to Him. You abide in God's love by keeping His commandments.

Application

1. Have you ever participated in a weight-loss program or fitness program? How long did it last?

2. If you have to see the end of the journey before you begin, you'll never start! God asks you only to take the next step with Him. What step is God asking you to take today?

Prayer

God, give me the heart and the faith to walk today in the ways You've prepared. Keep my eyes on You and guide my feet in straight paths. Amen.

53

INTERPOSITION

It is not always easy to sacrifice our time, our energy, and our possessions to meet the needs of others. It requires a love that is other-focused.

—Josh McDowell and Sean McDowell, *Sacrifice*

While waiting for a subway train in Brooklyn, a young college student fainted, falling onto the tracks in the deep well where trains speed by with amazing velocity. Without thinking, another commuter, a man on his way to work, jumped into the dangerous pit to help get her out moments before an oncoming train screeched to a halt. Escaping with only minor cuts and bruises, the student attributed her survival to the good Samaritan.[1]

The quick-witted commuter did what Zipporah did for Moses when she acted to prevent God's judgment. Interposition is when you act in obedience in an attempt to deflect God's judgment intended for someone else. The kingdom woman interposes herself between God and the natural consequences intended for another when she prays for a wayward child, when she intercedes on behalf of a failing spouse, or when she boldly acts in faith on behalf of a stranger. Like the commuter who leaped into action, she dares to surrender to God's revealed will even at a cost to herself.

Application

1. When, if ever, has someone in your life interposed herself or himself on your behalf (e.g., a relative, mentor, friend)?

2. On whose behalf is God calling you to interpose yourself today? How will you jump in to rescue another in obedience to God?

Prayer

Father, give me the courage to interpose myself for the sake of another. Give me courage to respond in obedience to You on behalf of one You love. Amen.

54

Steadfast Lovingkindness

Give thanks to the Lord, for he is good.
His love [chesed] endures forever.

—Psalm 136:1

The Inuit language has an unusually high number of words for "snow." One means "falling snow," another means "drifting snow," and so forth.[1] This people group whose livelihoods depend on describing local weather conditions accurately has developed an effective vocabulary for a condition that is crucial to their survival.

English-speaking Christians, who have been called to imitate God and reflect His love, use the word *love* to describe all kinds of affection. We use it to describe our affection for others, God's heart toward us, and even Christ's ultimate sacrifice on the cross. We even use it to describe how we feel about chocolate cake!

The original biblical languages, however, provide a much richer vocabulary for love. Specifically, the word the Hebrew scriptures use to describe God's steadfast love is *chesed*, which means "kind, generous, loyal, and unfailing." *Chesed* means kindness on steroids. It refers to a loyal love, whether or not the other party deserves it.[2] It's the solid commitment Rahab asked of God's spies, and it's the reliable love God offered to Rahab—and offers to us.

Application

1. Have you tasted God's steadfast, faithful love that doesn't fail? When in your life have you been most aware of God's radical kindness?

2. God longs for you to know His unfailing love in your deep places. Read Psalm 136. If you wrote your own psalm about God's goodness, what would your list include?

Prayer

God, I long to know Your chesed. *Fill me today with Your overwhelming kindness, and make me an instrument of Your* chesed *in the lives I touch today. Amen.*

55

God's Justice

So, from ancient times, the God of the Bible stood out from the gods of all other religions as a God on the side of the powerless, and of justice for the poor.

—Timothy Keller, *Generous Justice*

In his book *Generous Justice*, pastor and author Timothy Keller tells the story of a man he knew who owned a chain of car dealerships. His sales force, as was standard in the industry, was authorized to negotiate prices with customers. When the Christian business owner did some research, however, he discovered that men most often negotiated lower prices than women, and Anglos negotiated lower prices than people of color. This means that women of color, who were often poorer, were paying more for their cars than more affluent people. Recognizing the practice as unjust to those who most needed protection, he changed the company policy so that it was equally fair to all: The price on the sticker was the price people paid for the car.[1]

The man's concern about equity for the poor reflected God's own heart for justice. How much more will God—who is just, righteous, and compassionate—bring about justice for His elect (Luke 18:7–8). Throughout Scripture, God expresses a deep concern for the needs of widows, orphans, and aliens. The kingdom woman shares God's concern for the poor. And if she herself is poor, she is just the kind of instrument God chooses to use for His glory!

Application

1. Do you share God's heart for justice among the most vulnerable? What area of justice are you most passionate about?

2. Like the owner of the car dealership, you have choices on how to live. Is there a regular practice in your life that God might want to change to reflect His priorities? How will you respond?

Prayer

God, I praise You that You are a God whose eye is on the sparrow and whose hand upholds the weak. Give me wisdom and courage to reflect Your concern for the poor. Amen.

56

The Persistent Kingdom Woman

By perseverance the snail reached the ark.

—Charles Spurgeon, in *The Salt-Cellars*

Sometimes mothers can become overwhelmed by the needs of their families. The laundry needs to be done. One child needs new soccer cleats. Another child needs to go to the library to pick up a book for school. Another needs a haircut. Dishes begin to stack up in the sink. When many needs press in upon a woman, she *might* have the sense to prioritize and tackle the tasks that are most important. However, if one of her children is badgering her day after day, "I need to go to the library, I need to go to the library, I need to go to the library," that's most likely the task that will get done!

The story Jesus told about the unjust judge resonates in many ways with the situation of the burdened mother. The judge helped the woman seeking justice so that she would get off his back! But there's a twist to the story. At the end Jesus asked, "Will not God bring about justice for his chosen ones?" (Luke 18:7). Jesus was saying, in essence, "God is *not* like that unjust judge. In fact, He delights in executing justice for the ones He loves!"

Even when things don't look as if they will get better, we need to maintain contact with God, because prayer is to be an orientation, not a position. Tenacious prayer is a lifestyle that produces results. Prayer is more than getting on our knees or clasping our hands while closing our eyes. Prayer is an attitude of operating in conjunction with God.

As you go to God in prayer, go with the perseverance of the child who kept asking to go to the library, and the confidence that your God loves to give justice to those who ask.

Application

1. How does it make you feel when you have to beg for fair treatment? Have you felt slighted, overlooked, or denied justice?

2. What are you bringing to God's ear today? How are you being persistent in prayer?

Prayer

God, I thank You that You are a lover of justice. Give me the persistence of the overlooked widow, because I believe that You are good. Amen.

57

The Grand Illusion

All I have needed thy hand hath provided. / Great is thy faithfulness, / Lord, unto me.

—Thomas Chisholm, "Great Is Thy Faithfulness"

"Samantha" had been climbing the career ladder when, out of the blue, her company downsized, and she was let go from her job. About the same time, she discovered that her husband had had an affair and that her youngest child had been diagnosed with a learning disability. In no time, Samantha went from being on top of the world to being facedown on the carpet in prayer.

Samantha had been a woman who believed in the power of prayer. She knew that God could do miracles. She regularly told others of His goodness. However, like many of us, it wasn't until she had exhausted every other resource that she threw herself on God's mercy.

God welcomes us to come to Him in a posture of dependence. The witness of the Bible is that God *delights* in helping those who depend entirely on Him. Prayer isn't just for emergencies or when we need a breakthrough. Prayer is the everyday miracle where the God of the universe chooses to talk with us. And in this nearly inconceivable phenomenon, we find we can "approach the throne of grace with confidence, so that we may receive mercy and find grace to help us in our time of need" (Hebrews 4:16). It's what Jesus meant when He said we should be like little children (Matthew 18:3). It's the posture of the widow who petitions the unjust judge. It's the position of the single mother who begs God to provide a semester's tuition. When we depend entirely on God to meet our needs, we are truly in right relationship with Him.

Application

1. Has there been a time in your life when you needed to depend entirely on God? In what creative ways did God provide for you?

2. Today, are you in a season of plenty or want? In what ways are you looking to God for the resources you need?

Prayer

Father, teach me what it means to depend entirely on You. In times of abundant blessing and in times of desperate want, I put my trust in You. Amen.

58

Breath Prayer

At times our prayer may be
reduced to a single word: "Mercy!"
—Richard Foster, *Prayer*

When Jesus told the story of two men who went to the temple to pray—one a proud Pharisee and the other a humble sinner—He surprised His audience when He announced which of the men went home justified. It wasn't the religious man! Rather, it was the sinner who cried out, "God, have mercy on me, a sinner" (Luke 18:13). It wasn't the length of the prayer or eloquent words that moved the heart of God. It was the heart of one who humbly turned to Him.

This simple prayer is at the heart of the famous Jesus Prayer: "Lord Jesus Christ, Son of God, have mercy on me, a sinner." It's a prayer to be prayed not just once, or only on special occasions or in desperate circumstances, but with every breath we take. This kind of "breath prayer" is a short prayer whose cadence matches the natural rhythm of our breathing so that we can focus our mind on God. Repeated often, it can even become a way of praying unconsciously throughout the day. Other prayers to be breathed throughout the day might include "Come, Lord Jesus, come" or "I'm Yours" or "Speak, Lord." Prayer is a conversation, an attitude, a lifestyle. It can take different forms—verbal or written, silent or spoken, kneeling or standing. It's the act of taking ongoing opportunities to display our trust in the ability of the Savior to hear, understand, and deliver. Throughout your day, know that God hears every word you whisper to Him.

Application

1. What are you carrying in your heart right now? How are you expressing it to God through prayer?

2. Quiet your heart and ask the Spirit to reveal to you the simplest of prayers you might breathe to God. What do you hear?

Prayer

Lord Jesus Christ, Son of God, have mercy on me, a sinner. Speak Your word to my heart and bring words to my lips that I might converse with You throughout the day. Amen.

59

Getting Grounded

Let us run with perseverance the race marked out for us. Let us fix our eyes on Jesus, the author and perfecter of our faith.

—Hebrews 12:1–2

A common runner's injury, called plantar fasciitis, occurs when the tendons and ligaments on the bottom of the foot are damaged. This can be the result of a sudden blow or of overuse. With proper care, the injury is treatable. However, when left untreated, the condition can become chronic. During sleep, the connective tissues tighten so that walking first thing in the morning can be quite painful. This happens naturally with aging, too! The best thing an athlete or an aging person can do each morning is to rest her feet on the floor for five or ten minutes. This gently allows the feet to stretch and adjust before walking. In this, the sufferer is *grounded* before starting her day.

Prayer is to the Christian life what being physically grounded is to the life of the body.

When we pray, we connect ourselves to God in a way that impacts every movement we make throughout the day. Standing on God's Word, rooted in His promises, we're free to move through the world as those who are equipped. Prayer is a powerful tool in the hands of a kingdom woman. God often acts through people, even the people you would least suspect. He does it in cooperation with humanity. And He does it in answer to our prayers. Grounding ourselves in God isn't something we're meant to do *after* we're in crisis. Rather, the regular rhythm of prayer girds and strengthens us to run the good race so we're prepared when crises arise.

Application

1. What are some of the daily habits you *do not overlook?* Taking medication? Drinking water to stay hydrated? Eating three meals?

2. If prayer has been a challenge for you, as it is for many, how might you begin to integrate it into your daily routine in a sustainable way?

Prayer

Gracious God, You are the Rock on which I stand. Grant me the will and the discipline to ground myself in You and Your Word. Amen.

60

Access Granted

Jesus Christ went more willing to the cross,
than we do to the throne of grace.
—Thomas Watson, *The Christian Soldier*

At sporting events, concerts, or other public venues, the "talent"—whether athletes, musicians, or actors—often has access to a room or gathering space that is cloistered off from other attendees. To gain entrance to this space, public figures might be given a special badge or lanyard proclaiming "All Access Granted." With the pass, they often have access to food and other comforts that the general public does not.

As Christians, we don't come to God demanding access to His throne because *we say so*. Prayer is made possible through Christ alone; the only reason we can get to God is because the blood of Christ opened a door for us. Jesus said, "I am the way and the truth and the life" (John 14:6). He is the access point. We cannot enter into the presence of a holy God as sinful people. Access must be provided through the Son.

Have you been shivering out in the stadium on cold metal bleachers? Have you felt crushed by sweaty, roaring crowds pressing in on you? Too often we forget the gift Jesus has given us: to approach God with the assurance that we are welcome because of Christ.

Application

1. When you think of prayer, do you consider it more of an obligation or a privilege? Why?

2. Because you do have access to the throne of grace, what will you bring to God today?

Prayer

Thank You, God, that You have given me access to You through Your Son. In the strong name of Jesus, I humbly come before You this day. Amen.

61

Hidden Righteousness

Be careful not to do your "acts of righteousness" before [others], to be seen by them. If you do, you will have no reward from your Father in heaven.

—Matthew 6:1

Have you ever identified people who seem to enjoy being seen and noticed for their good works? It might be the woman who always finds a way to insert something into the conversation, such as, "I can't believe I broke a nail when I was serving at the shelter this morning." Or perhaps it's the woman who draws attention to herself, announcing at a church supper, "I guess I'm so tired because I wake up so early to be in prayer with the Lord." Or maybe it's the woman who flaunts her piety: "Can you believe it? All this fasting, and I'm still not losing weight!" Jesus warned against seeking this kind of notice.

If you spend more time trying to impress other people than you spend communicating with God in your private prayers, then your spiritual priorities are out of line. The *problem*, said Jesus, is that when we practice our righteousness in front of others, we lose our reward from God! The giving that pleases God is the kind no one else ever discovers, besides Him. The prayer that pleases God is the one done behind closed closet doors. The spiritual disciplines that please God aren't the kind others recognize as sacrificial, or even notice at all. What we do in secret is who we *really* are.

Your true faith shines through when you're alone.

Application

1. In what ways have you been tempted to let others see your good works?

2. Today, how can you serve, pray, or fast and keep it secret even from those who are closest to you?

Prayer

Father, I long to please only You. Teach me to serve for Your eyes alone. Teach me to pray for Your ears alone. Teach me to fast for Your notice alone. Amen.

62

GRATITUDE

The art of deep seeing makes gratitude possible.

—Ann Voskamp, *One Thousand Gifts*

Entertainment mogul Oprah Winfrey does it. Women of Faith speaker and best-selling author Ann Voskamp does it. Do you? Do you keep a journal of gratitude, expressing thankfulness for the blessings in your life? Contrary to popular opinion, this gratitude journal was someone else's idea entirely. The psalms are filled with songs and prayers of the faithful who recognize God as their good Provider. If you need a primer in prayers of thanksgiving, turn to Psalms!

Expressing our gratitude to God doesn't change God, but it does change *us*. Giving God thanks and praise reminds us that He is concerned about our needs. As we begin to open our eyes to the small blessings in our lives, we're given a bigger vision to recognize God at work.

Praise God when you have gas in your tank. Praise Him when the doctor says your illness is cured. Praise Him for that, but also praise Him because nothing went wrong today. Praise Him because He provides for your basic needs. Praise Him for the "fish" and the "bread." Praise Him for the ordinary. And guess what? He'll be there for the extraordinary.

Application

1. Are you in the habit of expressing your gratitude to God? In what ways?

2. If thankfulness isn't a regular part of your prayer life, begin today! What five things are you thankful for this day?

Prayer

God, You are the giver of all good gifts. Give me eyes to see Your abundant provision in my life and give me a heart of praise and gratitude to You. Amen.

63

Good, Not Best

Sever any tie in my heart except
the tie that binds my heart to Yours.

—David Livingstone, *Missionary Travels*, 1910

If our culture had a goddess of domesticity, it would be Martha Stewart. She prepares delicious meals from scratch, using ingredients most grocery stores don't even carry. She decorates her table with beautiful handmade creations. She designs and arranges her home so that every guest feels welcome and comfortable in an attractive setting. As Martha herself would say, "This is a good thing." It is. Offering hospitality to others is a very good thing. But it isn't necessarily the *best* thing.

If Martha Stewart's Old Testament counterpart is the busy and productive Proverbs 31 woman, then her New Testament counterpart is Lazarus's sister *Martha*. When Jesus and the disciples came to her house for dinner, Martha scrambled around making preparations. Feeling overwhelmed and resentful, she asked Jesus to tell her sister, Mary, to help her. The result, of course, was a teachable moment for Martha, not Mary.

The things that had distracted Martha weren't bad things. In fact, she was doing good things for Jesus. However, the very things Martha was doing *for* Jesus distracted her *from* Jesus. She'd become so involved with her agenda that she'd missed out on time with Christ. Gently, Jesus let Martha know—as He does us!—that being with Him was better (Luke 10:42).

Application

1. Do you naturally have more "Martha" in you or more "Mary"? What does this mean for you?

2. As Christ invites you to choose the best thing, what are some practical ways, this week, you can slow down to be with Him?

Prayer

God, I admit that I get carried away with my own work, busyness, and control. Help me to release my kitchen tools so that I can open my hands, eyes, and heart to You! Amen.

64

Schedule Strengthening

Don't try to work God into your schedule,
work your schedule around Him.
—Joyce Meyer, *Twenty-One Ways to Finding Peace and Happiness*

Most people remember to eat breakfast every day. They don't need to be reminded to shower. If an appointment is on their calendar, they show up for it. The things adults schedule into their days are the things that get done.

What routines do you follow without even thinking about them? Maybe you fix your hair and apply makeup every morning. Maybe you wash your face and brush your teeth at night. Or maybe you have a novel by the side of your bed that you like to pick up each night before you sleep.

In your personal life as a kingdom woman, it is essential to note that in the good things of life, you should try not to lose the important things. Look at your calendar, and it will show you your priorities. How you schedule your time, as well as your resources, reveals what is truly important to you.

Have you developed the habit of connecting with God? Do you anticipate it the way you look forward to joining your favorite television characters at the same time each week? You can be creative about how you do this. Write your devotional times into your schedule the way you'd pencil in a lunch date. Plan your commute to work around ways to hear from and talk to God. As you look at the natural rhythm of your weeks and days, how will you adjust your schedule around your commitment to show up for time with God?

Application

1. Are you, or have you ever been, in the regular habit of meeting with God? If you aren't now, what's holding you back?

2. Consider the kinds of resources you'll need to plan a regular time with the Lord: a Bible, another book, a journal, an MP3 recording of someone reading Scripture. What would be most useful to you?

Prayer

God, although I long to be with You, I've allowed my time to get eaten up by lesser things. Give me the strength to build new patterns of faithfulness to You. Amen.

65

Single-Minded

Jesus didn't finish everything His disciples wanted Him to do. . . . He did finish the work that God gave Him to do.

—Nancy Leigh DeMoss, *Lies Women Believe*

You probably know a woman like this. We'll call her "Jasmay." She's single, in her midforties, and was an ER nurse at a large university hospital when she had the opportunity to join her church on a missions trip to Appalachia. During the week she spent there, Jasmay sensed a calling from God to return, develop relationships with Christians there, and work alongside them in a ministry that promoted health and nutrition. Because Jasmay was *single*, she had the flexibility to arrange her schedule to gather supplies, travel back and forth, and equip local Christians to lead the ministry. Before this, being unmarried had left Jasmay feeling purposeless. But when she began to see how God was using her singleness to accomplish so much for the kingdom, Jasmay began to feel complete.

Following Christ is about offering to God

what we have been given. Singles offer their singleness, and married folks offer their marriedness. Retired widows offer themselves to God, and Christian teenagers offer themselves. Presidents of Fortune 500 companies offer what they have, and folks who've recently lost their jobs offer what they have. In the kingdom, there is no template for the type of person God will use. There is only the person who offers herself—whatever her circumstances—to be used as God sees fit. God desires you to be content where you are as a single. You have the opportunity that married women don't have to fully maximize your gifts, skills, time, treasures, and talents for the glory of God.

Application

1. Do you have, in your mind, a stereotype of the kind of person God uses? Are these stereotypes limiting what you do for God? Why or why not?

2. How do your stereotypes keep you from recognizing God's call on your life? What gifts of this season in your life can you offer to God?

Prayer

God, I give all that I am to You, and I trust that You will use all I am to Your glory. I offer myself, exactly as I am, to be an instrument of Your will and a builder of Your kingdom. Amen.

66

Abiding

Each day separately, all the day continually,
day by day successively, we abide in Jesus.
And the days make up the life.
—Andrew Murray, *Abide in Christ*

The Pennsylvania Convention Center is a massive structure located in the middle of Philadelphia's historic district. Expansive windows give visitors breathtaking views of Philadelphia's beautiful architecture. The venue is adjacent to restaurants, a hotel, and even mass-transit stations. As a result, those looking for shelter will often sit or lie down to sleep near an elevator or in a passageway. In fact, they find spots to rest the same way that tired travelers attending a conference or business meeting do! And yet if they're not sporting an admission badge or dressed in a fancy suit, these "loiterers" will get chased away by security. Those who are there for a purpose—to attend a concert or participate in an event—are allowed to stay, but those who are just hanging out are asked to move along.

To abide in God isn't to get in and get out. It

isn't like attending a business meeting and then hustling home to do what you *really* want to do. Abiding doesn't mean you simply pop in or pop out. *To abide* can be defined as "loitering" or "hanging out with." It implies a continual and ongoing connection while in the presence of another. It's to be like the man or woman, possibly without any other shelter, who quite literally has *no place better to be.*

Have you given yourself permission to linger? The temptation will always be to find something more "productive" to do. As you abide with God, the enemy will distract you a hundred different ways. God, however, invites you to *loiter* in his presence.

Application

1. What are your biggest distractions when you go to God in prayer? Are there a few predictable ones that come up again and again?

2. As you purpose to abide in God, how will you dismiss the nagging thoughts that tempt you to move along to more profitable ventures? What Scriptures might help?

Prayer

God, I reject the lie that time spent lingering with You is wasted. Today I cling to the truth that You have called me to holy loitering! Fix my eyes on You this day. Amen.

67

Holy Desire

Stop asking God to bless what you're doing.
Find out what God's doing. It's already blessed.

—Pastoral advice given to U2 rock star Bono,
in "Bono's American Prayer," *Christianity Today*

When children are small, they love eating treats. They devour cupcakes at preschool. They suck on lollipops after doctors' appointments. They beg for ice cream after baseball games. Often they "hunger" for sweets. The problem, of course, is that when mealtime comes, they're not hungry for wholesome foods. At some point, however, many children develop different desires. Perhaps when they notice how a diet of sweets makes them feel, they begin to hunger for healthier foods. Fresh fruits and vegetables, lean meats, and whole grains replace—in part!—a diet of junk food.

The kingdom woman who delights in the Lord begins to desire what the Lord desires. She opens her new home to visitors. She gives a friend a ride to work in the car God provides. She begins to *hunger* for those things that build God's kingdom.

Perhaps you still have an appetite for things that suit your own desires. As you spend time in His Word, learning what God desires, your hankerings will transform to match His.

Application

1. Which of your ongoing desires do *not* match God's desires?

2. In which areas of your life are the desires of your heart aligned with the desires of God's own heart?

Prayer

God, give me Your hunger for righteousness, mercy, and peace. Teach me to long for that which You desire. Amen.

68

Joy in the Storm

Or if on joyful wing, / cleaving the sky, / sun, moon, and stars forgot, / upward I fly, / still all my song shall be, / nearer, my God, to Thee.

—Sarah F. Adams, "Nearer, My God, to Thee"

On the corner of Cumberland Place and London Road in Southampton, England, stands a white stone memorial to the eight musicians who served on the infamous *Titanic*, which sank in 1912.

It's reported that when the ship began to sink, the musicians gathered in the first-class lounge to perform. Later they moved out onto the ship's deck to calm frantic passengers as they scrambled to board lifeboats. Many survivors have testified that the band continued to play until the very end. Though it's unclear which song was the *very* last one, many say that it was "Nearer, My God, to Thee." Former band members confirmed that playing this hymn had been the wish of bandleader Wallace Hartley, should a ship ever sink.[1]

If there was ever a time and place to be desperate, despondent, and without faith, the sinking of the *Titanic* was it. And yet, despite outward circumstances, Wallace Hartley displayed faith of another kind. It wasn't "happiness," which is a feeling experienced when things are going well. It was much closer to a very unique kind of *joy* the Bible describes. In the midst of panic and turmoil, joy is the supernatural calm and peace given by God's Spirit. It was given to Wallace Hartley, and he offered it to others. It's also promised to the kingdom woman who trusts in God.

Application

1. Do you know a Christian woman who faces difficult circumstances and yet continues to receive God's joy? What does that look like in her life?

2. In what areas of your life today are you lacking happiness? How can you receive the joy God is offering you?

Prayer

God, despite the circumstances I face, I find my life in You. Fill me today with a deep joy that comes from You. Amen.

69

The Cup Given

The cup which my Saviour giveth me,
can it be anything but a cup of salvations?
—Alexander MacLaren, *Week-Day Evening Addresses*

A preteen sits down beside her friends in the middle-school cafeteria. Unwrapping the sandwich her mother prepared—turkey and alfalfa sprouts on whole-grain wheat bread—and unpacking crunchy carrots and broccoli, she peers around to survey what others are eating. One student is enjoying hot, greasy pepperoni pizza. Another is tearing open a bag of potato chips. Yet another is gobbling down a package of miniature donuts. The girl gazes at the meals of other students with envy, wishing she'd been given something different.

It's tempting to do the same thing when we observe the lives of those around us. Many of us would gladly trade our marriages for the one next door that looks so storybook perfect. We envy the parents with successful, well-behaved children. We long for the kind of job that allows time and money for extravagant family vacations. When we look at our portion, many of us aren't too thrilled with what's in front of us.

The night before His crucifixion, seeing what had been laid before Him, Jesus prayed, "Father, if you are willing, take this cup from me; yet not my will, but yours be done" (Luke 22:42). The bitter cup wasn't removed from Jesus, and for many of us, it won't be removed either. Often, God asks us to eat and drink what is set before us. And as we do, we experience peace and are sustained by God the same way Jesus was.

Application

1. Many of us have wasted time wishing our lot were different than it is. What needs to change so can you avoid doing this in the future?

2. What has been set before you that God is asking you to bear today? Ask Him for strength to do His will.

Prayer

God, I receive the plate and cup that have been set in front of me. Give me strength this day to trust that You will sustain me just as You sustained Your Son, Jesus. Amen.

70

ATTITUDE

I am convinced that life is 10 percent what happens to me and 90 percent how I react to it.

—Chuck Swindoll

Chrystal had a difficult season in the life of her family. In the course of three months, her husband, Jessie was hospitalized three times. During this period, Chrystal faced countless stressors: caring for the couple's children, homeschooling them, supporting her husband in the hospital, worrying about financial concerns, coordinating a women's event and even leading worship.

And yet those who gathered to worship on Sunday morning looked to the front of the church and saw a woman they imagined having it all together. No doubt some, facing challenges of their own, having no idea what Chrystal was facing, would even have traded their own lots for hers!

None of us can trade our lives for someone else's. That's not a choice we've been given. As Chrystal's story reminds us, though, we *do* have a choice about the attitude with which we approach what is before us. As we allow God to shape our attitude, we become a reflection of his glory.

Application

1. Today, what is going on in your life that you would change, in a heartbeat, if you could?

2. As you choose to accept your circumstance, allow the Spirit to change your attitude about it. What prayerful phrase can you carry in your heart today about your situation?

Prayer

God, all that I face today is in Your hands. Though I cannot control what I will face, I do choose to face it with the attitude of Christ. Fill me with Your Spirit today. Amen.

71

Strength in Unity

Satan knows that whatever
he can divide, he can dominate.
—Tony Evans, *Kingdom Woman*

During America's Civil War, both Britain and France remained politically neutral. However, many industrialists in Europe were—for economic reasons—in favor of a quick Southern victory. When Abraham Lincoln's naval blockade restricted American cotton from being traded across the Atlantic, the price of cotton in France doubled, and many lost their jobs. So while the nations remained *officially* neutral, European profiteers supplied materials, arms, and even ships to the Confederacy to facilitate a Southern victory that would restore trade again. If the United States divided into two separate entities, European markets would benefit.

This is the same strategy Satan uses to defeat us today. If a woman is embroiled in conflict with a family member, Satan has won. If she spreads gossip at work, alienating her from coworkers,

Satan has won. If she instigates trouble in her church, Satan has won. Because God operates in a context of unity, Satan schemes to disrupt unity. The kingdom woman, however, aligns herself with the unity God has ordered.

Application

1. Are there relationships in your life today that are under attack by Satan's schismatic schemes?

2. What practical choices will you make to live in the unity God has designed?

Prayer

God, help me to recognize the plans of Satan to divide and conquer. Give me wisdom and strength to align myself with Your purposes this day, for Your glory. Amen.

72

Humble Obedience

The more humble a man is in himself, and the more obedient towards God, the wiser will he be in all things, and the more shall his soul be at peace.

—Thomas à Kempis, *The Imitation of Christ*

About the time a child is two or three years of age, she learns to wield—sometimes quite fiercely!—the word *no*. Often the child will test every limit the parent sets. What the child doesn't realize, however, is that her stubborn disobedience can threaten her safety. If she doesn't yield to a parent's "*STOP*!" at a busy street corner, or if she doesn't halt when told to back away from a fiery stovetop, she places herself at great risk. Humbly, she has to learn to trust that her caregiver can see more than she can see. She will be best suited to a life of health and wellness when she learns to obey the voice that lovingly puts boundaries around her behavior.

The kingdom woman who humbly learns to trust God's voice—obeying God's "Stop" and

God's "Go," God's "Yes" and God's "No"—will enjoy a soul at peace. She may not always understand *why* or even agree with God's instructions, but as she obeys, she will be conformed more and more into the image of Christ, a useful tool in the hand of the Master.

Application

1. Submitting to God's will can be downright difficult. Have you ever agreed to humbly obey God when you would rather have not?

2. When you've obeyed God despite your own inner resistance, what fruit have you seen from that obedience?

Prayer

God, in my flesh I'm prone to disregard Your voice and go my own way. Give me a heart that longs to humbly obey You and the will to respond faithfully to Your voice. Amen.

73

Father Look-Alikes

Just as we have borne the likeness of the earthly man, so shall we bear the likeness of the man from heaven.

—1 Corinthians 15:49

Airports are some of the best places to people watch. It's fascinating to sit beside a busy passageway and observe the variety of folks who pass by. It's always interesting to see *families* tromp along together. If a couple is traveling with several children or teens, it can be fun to search for family resemblances. Does a small boy resemble his father? Does a teenage girl walk or smile or talk like her mother? Sometimes a young child or teen will be the spitting image of one of his or her parents!

Just as each of us bears some resemblance to the ones who formed us, so too were we made to reflect the image of God. As we practice obedience to God, we begin to resemble Christ more and more. As our hands feed the hungry, they begin to match His. As our feet are swift to deliver the good news to others, they match Christ's own feet. As our ears listen to the cries of the needy, they match the ears of Jesus. As our eyes recognize the image of God in others, they match His eyes. When we submit ourselves to God's shaping process, others who witness our lives will remark how much we resemble our Brother, Jesus, and our Father, God.

Application

1. Do others remark that you look like one of your biological parents? In what way? If you don't know one of your parents, in what ways do you imagine you resemble them?

2. When others look at your life, do they recognize the eyes and ears, hands and feet, heart and mind of Jesus Christ? Explain.

Prayer

God, I believe that I have been created to bear Your holy image. Work in my heart and mind today so that I might faithfully represent Christ to the world. Amen.

74

Holy Submission

Some day my prince will come. / Some day we'll meet again, / and away to his castle we'll go / to be happy forever I know.

—"Some Day My Prince Will Come," *Snow White*

Some girls create something called a "hope chest" during their childhood, adolescence, and young adulthood, in which they place symbols of their hopes and dreams for the future. A girl might put any number of items inside her hope chest: a magazine picture of her dream wedding dress, a piece of lace from her mother's wedding veil, a swatch of fabric she likes, or pictures of a garden she'd like to create. In the end, though, no amount of planning and preparing can magically conjure the future she desires.

Many women can be tempted to try to control the future they long for. They may believe that by applying themselves in school, they can earn the dream job. They might hope that by wearing the right clothes or attending the right gatherings, they will woo Prince Charming. Perhaps they've planned out the order, spacing, and sexes of their children before they've even married! Though it's natural to imagine what the future may hold, a kingdom woman holds her hopes and dreams for the future lightly. Confident that her life is in God's hands, she waits patiently for Him to unfold the future He has planned for her.

Application

1. When you were younger, how did you imagine your future? Did it pan out the way you imagined?

2. Today, what aspect of the future are you tempted to try to manipulate? How will you release this into God's care today?

Prayer

God, I trust my past, my present, and my future to You. Though I do dream of what the future may hold, give me patience and trust to submit myself to Your will for my life. Amen.

75

TRUE SATISFACTION

The human spirit is never satisfied in a lasting way by anything less than God.

—Billy Graham, *Just as I Am*

Though we were made to find satisfaction in God alone, we're often tempted to seek it everywhere *except* in Him. If we've going to move into a new home, we can be tempted to believe that choosing the right cabinets and countertops will satisfy us. If we're single, we might think that finding the "right" man will satisfy. If we long to have children, we might think that when we have a baby we'll *finally* be satisfied. If we're climbing the career ladder, we might believe that a certain opportunity or salary would, at last, satisfy. No matter how much we acquire and achieve, something always seems just out of our reach.

We aren't satisfied, claims Billy Graham, because "we cannot be satisfied with anything less than God."[1] So while a purchase or relationship or achievement might sooth our longings for a moment, only God will truly satisfy the deepest desires of our hearts. It's like chewing on a piece of sugary bubblegum and expecting to be nourished and filled and strengthened.

Notice today the gnawing inside of you to be fully satisfied. As you resist turning to natural sources for satisfaction—the refrigerator or wine glass or television screen—you allow God to fill you with himself.

Application

1. What popular "fillers" do you habitually turn to for satisfaction? Food? Busyness? Entertainment? Various substances?

2. As you agree to be filled by God alone, which alternate sources of satisfaction will you release this week? Share your resolve with one friend.

Prayer

God, I believe that You created my soul with a hunger to be satisfied. Give me strength to turn away from my soothers and addictions so that I might be filled by Your Spirit. Amen.

76

Love Drives Out Fear

The person who loves God with his whole heart has no fear of death or judgment or hell, because perfect love gives certain access to God.

—Thomas à Kempis, *The Imitation of Christ*

A number of years after Jesus' resurrection and ascension, the early church was trying to figure out what it looked like to live faithfully for God. During that period, John wrote to believers, instructing them how to live. He wrote, "There is no fear in love. But perfect love drives out fear, because fear has to do with punishment. The one who fears is not made perfect in love" (1 John 4:18).

All of us, naturally, live with some degree of fear. Some of us are concerned about our jobs or house payments. Others may harbor anxieties about health or family concerns. And though most days it's not on our minds, we might even have a quiet, lingering fear of death. The world offers a number of solutions for our fears. It suggests that the right investment banker or doctor or life coach will teach us how to live without fear.

The Scriptures, however, declare that what casts out fear is *love*. Your love for God, and God's love for you, are what set you free from all fear.

APPLICATION

1. Are you prone to fear and anxiety? What things do you worry about most often?

2. God invites you to release your fear to Him and be filled with His perfect love. What are two or three scriptures to which you can cling in this process?

PRAYER

God, I trust that Your perfect love casts out all fear. Teach me to trust in You. Fill me with Your love that never fails. Amen.

77

Loving God

Love God, and He will enable you to love others, even when they disappoint you.

—Francine Rivers, *And the Shofar Blew*

The Pharisees, trying to trap Jesus, sent a law expert to try to trip Jesus up. "Teacher," he queried, "which is the greatest commandment in the Law?" (Matthew 22:36). It was the kind of question, they thought, that would give them ammunition against Jesus. In response to their request for a single commandment, Jesus gave them *two*: *Love God and love your neighbor*! These two commandments, Jesus taught, couldn't be separated from each other.

Our love of God is expressed *as* we love our neighbor. The two can't be pulled apart. When the neighbor we're called to love is a kindly older woman or a cute little toddler, the commandment to love feels mostly manageable. But when we're called to love a neighbor who disrespects us or a spouse who's been unfaithful, or to pray in hope for a wayward child, we may find ourselves lacking in will and ability.

Thankfully, God doesn't ask us to love on our own. God helps us, enables us, to love the one who is difficult.

Application

1. Whom in your life today do you find most difficult to love? Why?

2. As you think of this person, invite God to help you to love him or her. What do you hear God speaking to your heart?

Prayer

God, You have created me to love You and others. Help me today to love the ones who are most difficult to love, letting Your love flow through me. Amen.

78

Wings of Safety

God is not an employer looking for employees. He is an Eagle looking for people who will take refuge under his wings.

—John Piper, *A Sweet and Bitter Providence*

When a newborn comes home from the hospital, she is entirely helpless. She depends on her parents to do *everything* for her. Unable to protect or defend herself, she is completely vulnerable. A mother takes this little one, wraps her in a blanket, and snuggles her close to her chest. The image is one of complete security.

It's easy to forget that this is God's posture toward us! One of the images Scripture uses to describe God is the eagle who gathers its eaglets under protective wings (Psalm 91:4). We, who are dependent and vulnerable, are tucked under God's feathered wing. It's a place of warmth and security.

Perhaps the circumstances in your life right now leave you feeling vulnerable. You may feel as though you need a strong protector. Quiet your heart, close your eyes—maybe even curl up in a blanket!—and picture the near presence of God shielding and protecting you.

Tucking yourself under God's wing isn't just for quiet moments either. God guards you like a mother eagle when you step out to share your faith with others, as you serve those around you, and even as you face life's difficulties. In fact, there isn't a single moment when you're *not* tucked next to the heart of God.

Application

1. What life circumstance is making you feel vulnerable right now?

2. As you prayerfully nestle into God's bosom, what scripture helps you settle into the peace and security He offers?

Prayer

Father, too often I forget I'm held in Your protective embrace. This day, remind me that You are the One in whom I find my strength. Amen.

79

Faith of Your Own

You are God's woman. You are not called to sit by the window waiting for God to send you a husband. You had better have some faith yourself and believe God down in your own spirit.

—T. D. Jakes, *Woman, Thou Art Loosed!*

During different seasons of a woman's life, she might be tempted to set her hopes on someone other than God. The single woman might long for a godly husband to meet her needs. The married woman might secretly wish that her husband would step up and take responsibility for the spiritual welfare of their household. The widowed woman might long, wistfully, for the good old days when her husband initiated family prayer. Though there's nothing wrong with "coming together before the Lord," women can be tempted to avoid, or postpone, intimacy with God.

However, the kingdom woman, whatever her marital status, knows that she is *God's woman.* She understands that God has called her to know

Him, trust Him, and respond to Him. Instead of waiting for someone else to be the bridge that connects her to God—a partner or a pastor or a teacher—she pursues God and expects Him to use her as an agent of His kingdom.

Application

1. Describe a time in your life when you wanted to rely on someone else to be your "bridge" to the Lord.

2. Do you view yourself as someone uniquely called and gifted to be used by God? How is God calling you to use your unique gifts today?

Prayer

God, I'm reminded that I am Your woman and that You have great plans for me. I give myself to You to be used to build Your kingdom. Amen.

80

A Living Church

Going to church on Sunday does not make you a Christian any more than going into a garage makes you an automobile!

—Attributed to Billy Sunday

Many critics of the church cite the behavior of Christians as the source of their doubt. They see Christians dressing up for church on Sunday morning but abusing substances, or each other, on Saturday night. They witness people who carry Bibles also carrying heavy loads of judgment for those whose behavior falls short of their standards. They notice that those who claim to be saved by Jesus seem to have little concern for those who need to be saved from hunger, poverty, and violence. This is far from true of all Christians, of course, but it's true of those who show up at church on Sunday morning to feel a little better.

Although many today think of church as the building with a steeple that's used a few hours a week, Jesus had something very different in mind. The Greek word *ecclesia* suggests that the church is a living organism, a body whose purpose is to bring God's rule on earth as it is in heaven. The type of person God desires has a heart that is open to becoming a disciple of Jesus and ushering in His kingdom. This is the person who's willing to follow Jesus 24-7-365, not just on Sundays. It's the person who is being transformed each day into one who bears the image of Christ.

Application

1. Describe a time in your life, either before you knew Christ personally or since, when church was more of a habit than a relationship. Explain.

2. What about today? How are you functioning as a member of the living, breathing body of Christ?

Prayer

God, I believe that You have called me to function under Your headship. Guide and direct each movement of my heart, mind, and body each moment of each day. Amen.

81

Memorable Last Words

As we teach others to love and obey Jesus, we are fulfilling His command to make disciples.

—Francis Chan and Mark Beuving, *Multiply*

A somber family gathers to hear the reading of the last will and testament of its patriarch, recently deceased. His wife had preceded him in death by just nine months. The wealthy man had been the father of three and the grandfather of seven. One of his children was a successful surgeon. The second was a recovering addict, in and out of rehab facilities for decades. The man's third child was an adult with severe physical and developmental disabilities, living in an institution. As the attorney of the man's estate shuffled papers, the room was otherwise silent. Each family member wondered what he or she might, or might not, receive. Would the man be generous to all three children? Would he give his money to charity? No one knew.

Like the parent who hollers last-minute instructions to her school-age child—"Button your coat! Take your lunch!"—the very last thing this man would say, through a legal document, would reveal what he valued most.

Before His ascension into heaven, Jesus spoke these memorable last words to underscore His own priorities: "All authority in heaven and on earth has been given to me. Therefore go and make disciples of all nations, baptizing them in the name of the Father and of the Son and of the Holy Spirit, and teaching them to obey everything I have commanded you. And surely I am with you always, to the very end of the age" (Matthew 28:18–20).

Application

1. As a Christian, have you taken seriously Jesus' command to make disciples? Explain.

2. Ask God to show you one or two women with whom you might share the gospel, or someone He may want you to disciple.

Prayer

God, thank You for blessing me on my journey with women and men who have discipled me. Now use me to nurture and feed another disciple of Jesus. Amen.

82

Training

If they follow Jesus, men escape from the hard yoke of their own laws, and submit to the kindly yoke of Jesus Christ.

—Dietrich Bonhoeffer, *The Cost of Discipleship*

When a woman teaches a girl how to knit, she uses thick needles that are the right size for a child's hands and coordination. The same is true for the yarn. Sitting beside the girl, she slowly knits a few stitches of her own to show the girl how it's done. Then casting yarn onto the girl's needles, she helps guide the girl's hands to take a stitch or two. When the girl thinks she can do it on her own, she attempts to make her own first loose stitches. The experienced knitter continues to sit by her side and guide her as her mind and body learn the rhythms of knitting.

Too often, when it comes to discipleship, we expect that with the right tools and a detailed pattern, like knitting a sweater, a young woman should be able to clothe herself in Christ on her own! The model shared in Titus, however, is one in which the older woman acts as a shepherd to the younger one. She sits and walks beside her as she becomes accustomed to the rhythms of discipleship. She helps the new Christian understand the pattern—the one prescribed in God's Word—that often needs a bit of explanation. The older woman invites the younger one to look over her shoulder as she patterns her own life after Jesus. This training is so thorough that when it's complete, the younger believer can share it with someone else who wants to learn the ropes.

Application

1. From whom have you learned how to follow Jesus? How did they teach you?

2. As you invest in discipling newer Christians, what do you feel is most important for their growth and development in following Christ?

Prayer

God, I didn't get to where I am today on my own. Thank You for those saints who led me to You. Teach me to give myself to others just as You poured Your life into teaching Your friends. Amen.

83

Uncontrolled Tongue

The tongue also is a fire, a world of evil among the parts of the body. It corrupts the whole person, sets the whole course of his life on fire, and is itself set on fire by hell.

—James 3:6

"Have you heard about Cora, bless her heart? I'm so concerned about her. This isn't gossip either. In fact, I only mention her soap-opera addiction and failing marriage and imprisoned son so that we can pray for her. Bless her heart. Remember, you didn't hear this from me!"

Do you know anyone like this? The woman with a loose tongue is more interested in letting other folks know what she knows—while trying to scratch some more dirt out of them—than she is in inviting another hurting woman to join her for lunch or accompanying the hurting friend to visit her son in prison. And all her gossip is thinly disguised in the name of prayer! Though she intends to reveal something about another person, she actually exposes her true nature when she overshares.

Mature kingdom women have no need to pass along anything that doesn't build others up. If a situation is truly critical, she *prays* about it rather than talking about praying about it. She *engages* with the woman who is suffering or sinning. She breaks confidence only as her prayers rise to the ears of the Father.

Application

1. When you've encountered women who gossip, have you shared your deepest difficulties and troubles with them? Why?

2. Do others know you as a trustworthy kingdom woman? What are some signs that others feel they can entrust their cares and concerns to you?

Prayer

God, I recognize that the tongue You gave me is a powerful tool. Teach me to tame it and use it for praise and prayer that glorifies You and blesses others. Amen.

84

Holy Response

Like our fellow sisters . . . we have power to bury this evil called slavery once and for all.

—Shayne Moore and Kimberly McOwen Yim, *Refuse to Do Nothing*

When a new friend invited Kimberly Yim, a young mom, to view a movie about modern-day human trafficking called *Call + Response*, Kimberly accepted. She recalls, "When the film was over I could barely lift my head. My eyes fought back tears. I was surprised by what I had seen and the effect it had had on me."[1] That experience stayed with Kimberly, and she responded to the film's invitation to get involved. What began as a search for answers on her computer became her life's work to educate others and eradicate slavery.

Though many are emotionally moved by tragic circumstances, Kimberly *responded* by following in the footsteps of Queen Esther. Recognizing injustice in the world, each gathered her courage and acted on behalf of the oppressed. Esther even risked her life to secure freedom for her people.

Though we might be tempted to fictionalize someone like Esther—elevating her as if she's the heroine in a make-believe fairy tale—she was a flesh-and-blood woman with doubts and fears, just like us. Today God is raising up kingdom women like Esther and Kimberly, who will use their voices as instruments of His justice in the world. Are you one of them?

Application

1. As you think back over your life, have you ever been emotionally moved by some injustice? How did you respond?

2. Today, how are you participating in building God's kingdom on earth as it is in heaven as an agent of His justice?

Prayer

God, thank You for the freedoms I enjoy, small and large. Grant me courage to stand, like Queen Esther, on behalf of those who cannot defend themselves. Come, Holy Spirit! Amen.

85

IMPERFECT AGENT

A kingdom woman is not a perfect woman. She is a forgiven woman.

—Chrystal Evans Hurst, *Kingdom Woman*

The Samaritan woman Jesus met at the well was, by her culture's standards, *all wrong*. In a society with rigid relational taboos, she was, in relation to Jesus, the wrong gender, the wrong religion, and the wrong race. Yet this was the woman God would use to spread the good news about Jesus and the kingdom He ushered in.

If God chose a woman today who was *all wrong* in the eyes of the world, what would she look like? Perhaps she'd be an exotic dancer at a strip club. Maybe she'd be a woman living in poverty. Maybe she'd be a woman battling an addiction. She would most certainly not fit in with the well-heeled Sunday-morning crowd in many churches.

When we limit God to using the women *we* think He should use—those who are influential, educated, well dressed, or well-spoken—we limit the plans and possibilities He desires. Yes, the women God chooses include very unlikely ones, like the woman at the well. They also include women just like you, who simply may not be confident in all they bring to the table as bearers of good news. The kingdom woman isn't perfect, but she is forgiven. She is *you.*

Application

1. What are your fears about God calling you to share your faith with others?

2. How has God supplied your needs in the past and equipped you for ministry? How is He doing this now?

Prayer

God, I admit that I have at times believed Your call is for other women. Today I offer myself—imperfect but forgiven!—to be used as Your bearer of good news. Amen.

86

The Time Is Now

When I stand before God at the end of my life, I would hope that I would not have a single bit of talent left, and could say, "I used everything you gave me."

—Erma Bombeck

Every December, advertisements for health clubs and weight-loss programs ramp up in the media. companies know that Americans are eating too much food, and come January 1, many will get serious—for as much as three or four weeks—about living differently and will make a resolution to lose weight. Those who struggle to maintain a healthy weight know the temptation of the "I'll start tomorrow" syndrome. But tomorrow never comes! Instead, every day becomes the last day for bingeing. Because tomorrow is always somewhere off in the future, no action takes place today that leads to a healthier tomorrow.

This is the same temptation many Christians face when it comes to telling others how much God has done for them. They may feel as though there's simply too much to do at home. Perhaps their load at work feels overwhelming. They might even be convinced that they need more theological training to tell others about Jesus. There are many excuses to use.

Remember that God's time is *now*. Just as it is with eating healthy food or exercising regularly, the woman who succeeds isn't the one who *intends* to do it tomorrow. It's the woman who is compelled to share the good news of Jesus *today* with those around her.

Application

1. Have you known someone whose enthusiasm for sharing Jesus was contagious? Describe her.

2. This week, how might you share your faith with someone God loves? What is one practical step you can take today?

Prayer

God, I give You thanks and praise for Jesus. Send Your Spirit to ignite my heart with a passion for Him and His message. Give me Your courage to proclaim Him boldly. Amen.

87

Impact

From the very beginning women share God's command for humans to rule, subdue, and manage this earth. They are co-regents.

—Gary Thomas, *Sacred Influence*

When a child is very young, her friendships are often a matter of convenience. She might play dolls with a neighbor across the street, swim with the family next door, or go to the park with someone from church. When she gets a bit older, however, she begins to choose her own friends. The first time she brings home a friend from school for a playdate, her parents may size up the new child to decide what kind of an influence this child might be. Will this new friend make a positive or negative impact on their child? A kingdom woman might even be asking, "How will my child impact the life of her friend?"

The kingdom woman, and the kingdom family, are meant to impact others. Instead of being shaped by the world—culture, media, and so on—the kingdom woman is responsible for shaping the world in which she lives. In her family, church, and community, she is a preview of all God offers and can supply. When people of the world look at her, they know what the character of God is like.

Application

1. In the course of your day, who are the people you make the greatest impact on?

2. In what ways will you shine forth the character of God today? Whose lives will be impacted by your witness?

Prayer

God, thank You for the holy privilege of representing You to the world. Give me grace to shine Your light and reflect Your glory this day. Amen.

88

Jesus Follower

It may seem that there are many followers of Jesus. . . . It seems to me there is a more suitable word to describe them. They are not followers of Jesus. They are fans of Jesus.

—Kyle Idleman, *Not a Fan*

No matter where you live, you'll find some over-the-top crazy sports fans. Students who are wild for the Duke Blue Devils paint themselves from head to toe in royal-blue paint. Fans of the Chicago Blackhawks will strip down to almost nothing except a black-and-red logo tattooed to their chests. One Dallas Cowboys fan wears a blue Mohawk with the iconic blue star painted on the side of his head. And, of course, fierce mamas of dancing ballerinas wear . . . pink.

People can have a lot of passion and energy as fans of athletes, musicians, movie stars, and even . . .Jesus. Even some Christians can be very enthusiastic about who Jesus is and yet fail to pattern their lives after Him. They may think He's wonderful but never quite move from being fans to being followers. The life of a follower looks a lot like the life of Jesus. Followers move toward the sick, the weak, and the broken. They feed the hungry. They proclaim the goodness of God and His kingdom. They spend time with sinners, whom the religious despise.

It's easy to be a fan. If your faith leaves you very comfortable, you might just be one. The kingdom woman, however, is willing to sacrifice comfort and privilege as she follows in the footsteps of Jesus.

Application

1. Do you know people who like to talk about Jesus but never get their hands dirty with the business of ministering to others?

2. In what ways is God inviting you to follow in Jesus' footsteps today?

Prayer

God, give me the courage to move from the comfort of being Your fan to following the way of Jesus with my heart, soul, mind, and strength. Amen.

89

God Pleasers

Man corrupt everything, say Shug. He on your box of grits, in your head, and all over the radio. He try to make you think he everywhere. Soon as you think he everywhere, you think he God. But he ain't.

—Alice Walker, *The Color Purple*

As young children, we may have tried to please our parents in the way we behaved. When we started school, we may have become more concerned with the opinions of our peers. Suddenly, what mattered most was what *others* thought of us. As we moved into adolescence, we may have tried to win the affection of a romantic interest. As adults, we may seek to please a spouse if we're married. Or perhaps an employer. Throughout our lives, we seek to be acceptable in the eyes of others in many ways.

The temptation for many of us is to allow other people—whose opinions matter *deeply* to us—to replace God. We begin to perform for their eyes rather than to please the Lord. But in the end, no matter how hard we try to please others, they are *not* God.

The kingdom woman focuses the eyes and ears of her heart on the heavens. Her eyes search for the smile on God's face. Her ears are tuned in to the sound of His voice. Pleasing God is the single greatest desire of her heart. Is it yours?

Application

1. Whom in your life do you try very hard to please? An employer? A church leader? A family member?

2. Sometimes pleasing and serving others does please God. But often we're only seeking the approval of others. In what ways are you striving to win the praise and approval of people instead of God?

Prayer

God, it's the desire of my heart to please You alone. Today I turn toward You, seeking Your face and listening for Your voice. Teach me to delight in Your opinion of me. Amen.

90

Striving to the End

Then let us all do what is right, strive with all our might toward the unattainable, develop as fully as we can the gifts God has given us, and never stop learning.

—Ludwig van Beethoven

Ludwig van Beethoven, who lived at the turn of the nineteenth century, is known as one of the world's most famous composers. As he was growing up in Bonn, Germany, his father taught him to play the piano and compose. At the age of twenty-two, he moved to Vienna, Austria, and began to study with Joseph Haydn. When Beethoven was thirty, however, his hearing began to fail, and by the end of his life, he was almost completely deaf. What seems almost incomprehensible is that many of Beethoven's most beloved works were composed during this period when he was unable to hear them! Until the very end of his life, Beethoven continued to use the gifts God had given him.

Despite her outward circumstances, the kingdom woman continues to strive, throughout her days, to become the woman God has made her to be. Though health may fail, though finances may be tight, though heartbreak may come, she keeps offering herself to God as the woman through whom He will touch the world He loves.

You are that kingdom woman! Bless you as you continue to become all that the King has made you to be!

Application

1. Describe someone you know or have heard about who, like Beethoven, continued using the gifts God gave him or her until the end of life.

2. How are you continuing to grow in the gifts God has given you? What are you doing to develop those gifts?

Prayer

God, I believe that I am Your woman. Fill me today so that I might continue to strive to serve You and usher in the kingdom Jesus established. Amen.

Notes

Devo 5

1. *Strong's Concordance*, s.v. Hebrew 5828 "*ezer*," http://biblesuite.com/hebrew/5828.htm.

Devo 6

1. Sojourner Truth, "Ain't I a Woman?" (speech, Women's Rights Convention, Akron, Ohio, 1851), accessed April 16, 2013, http://en.wikisource.org/wiki/Ain%27t_I_a_Woman%3F.

Devo 11

1. Yankelovich market research data, cited in Louise Story, "Anywhere the Eye Can See, It's Likely to See an Ad," *New York Times*, January 15, 2007, accessed April 18, 2013, http://www.nytimes.com/2007/01/15/business/media/15everywhere.html?pagewanted=all&_r=0.

Devo 18

1. Joni and Friends, "Joni's Bio," accessed March 19, 2013, http://www.joniandfriends.org/jonis-corner/jonis-bio/; and Joni Eareckson Tada, *Joni. An Unforgettable Story* (Grand Rapids, MI: Zondervan, 2001), 13–18, 125.

Devo 24

1. Mother Teresa probably adapted this from Kent M. Keith's "The Paradoxical Commandments."

Devo 33

1. *Strong's Concordance*, s.v. Greek 3056 "*logos*," http://biblesuite.com/greek/3056.htm.
2. *Strong's Concordance*, s.v. Greek 4487 "*rhema*," http://biblesuite.com/greek/4487.htm.
3. Adapted from Frank Pastore, *Shattered: Struck Down, but Not Destroyed* (Carol Stream, IL: Tyndale, 2010), 158; an interview with Gina Pastore, May 2, 2012.

Devo 36

1. C. S. Lewis, *Mere Christianity* (New York: HarperCollins, 2001), 128.

Devo 49

1. Rosa Parks, quoted in Donnie Williams, with Wayne Greenhaw, *The Thunder of Angels: The Montgomery Bus Boycott and the People Who Broke the Back of Jim Crow* (Chicago:Lawrence Hill Books, 2006), 48.

Devo 50

1. *The Wizard of Oz*, directed by Victor Fleming (Metro-Goldwyn-Mayer, 1939).

Devo 53

1. Shayna Jacobs, "Hero Saves Woman Who Falls onto Subway Tracks," *New York Daily News*, August 29, 2012, accessed April 18, 2013, http://www.nydailynews.com/new-york/hero-saves-woman-falls-subway-tracks-article-1.1147542.

Devo 54

1. David Robson, "There Really Are 50 Eskimo Words for 'Snow,' " *Washington Post*, January 14, 2013, http://articles.washingtonpost.com/2013-01-14/national/36344037_1_eskimo-words-snow-inuit.
2. *Strong's Concordance*, s.v. Hebrew 1136 "*chesed*," http://biblesuite.com/hebrew/1136.htm.

Devo 55

1. Timothy Keller, *Generous Justice* (New York: Dutton, 2010), 111.

Devo 68

1. Steve Turner, *The Band That Played On: The Extraordinary Story of the Eight Musicians Who Went Down with the* Titanic (Nashville: Thomas Nelson, 2011); and Joey Butler, "Did Faith Drive Titanic Musicians?" The United Methodist Church

(UMC.org), April 15, 2011, http://www.umc.org/site/apps/nlnet/content3.aspx?c=lwL4KnN1LtH&b=5259669&ct=9353535.

Devo 75

1. Billy Graham, *Just As I Am*, (New York: HarperCollins, 1997), 729.

Devo 84

1. Shayne Moore and Kimberly McOwen Yim, *Refuse to Do Nothing: Finding Your Power to Abolish Modern-Day Slavery* (Downers Grove, IL: InterVarsity, 2013), 39.